To: Jenny
from: Jen

MW01253107

Jenny,

thank you for everything you
have done for me. You and
your family are a blessing
in my life. God bless you!

Love you guys!
Jessica
☺

02-2015

More of You, *Less of me*

Christina Lane

BALBOA
PRESS
A DIVISION OF HAY HOUSE

Balboa Press books may be ordered through booksellers or by contacting:

Balboa Press
A Division of Hay House
1663 Liberty Drive
Bloomington, IN 47403
www.balboapress.com
1 (877) 407-4847

Because of the dynamic nature of the Internet, any web addresses or
links contained in this book may have changed since publication and
may no longer be valid. The views expressed in this work are solely those
of the author and do not necessarily reflect the views of the publisher,
and the publisher hereby disclaims any responsibility for them.

The author of this book does not dispense medical advice or prescribe the use
of any technique as a form of treatment for physical, emotional, or medical
problems without the advice of a physician, either directly or indirectly. The
intent of the author is only to offer information of a general nature to help
you in your quest for emotional and spiritual well-being. In the event you use
any of the information in this book for yourself, which is your constitutional
right, the author and the publisher assume no responsibility for your actions.

Any people depicted in stock imagery provided by Thinkstock are models,
and such images are being used for illustrative purposes only.
Certain stock imagery © Thinkstock.

Printed in the United States of America.

ISBN: 978-1-4525-8718-9 (sc)
ISBN: 978-1-4525-8719-6 (hc)
ISBN: 978-1-4525-8717-2 (e)

Library of Congress Control Number: 2013920740

Balboa Press rev. date: 12/13/2013

Dedicated to God, for never giving up on me,
and for loving and saving me from myself
through my amazing husband and children.

*… He who has begun a good work in you will
complete it until the day of Jesus Christ.*

Philippians 1:6 (NKJV)

To God be all the Glory

My first thanks goes to God. Without Him, I would not be here today. I am so grateful for His love for me, for how He worked *all* things out for my good. He never gave up on me and gently nudged me in this direction. *Lord, there are no words that could ever describe what I feel for You in my heart. What You have made possible for me in my life leaves me in total awe. I am forever grateful to You. Thank You.*

Rob, I don't even know where to begin. We have been through so much in our twenty years together. Through the challenges, through the heartache and through the crazy, fun and silly times, we have persevered. We have tried to leave one another, we have tried to remove one another from each other's lives, but to no avail. The storms we have weathered and the challenges we have fought through have brought us, as crazy as it seems, closer to God and to each other. We have gained understanding and, most of all, we have learned what God's love really means. At times, I'm amazed how our marriage has survived the struggles we have ploughed through. It proves to me that we have built our marriage on solid ground. Reminds me of Matthew 7:24-25. Rob, I would not want to have taken this journey with anyone else. I thank you for your love, kindness and generosity, and for the lessons I have learned through sharing our life together. I look forward to what God has in store for our future. May we cling to Him with all that we are. Thank you for your willingness to allow me to share our story with others. To share our experience, our struggles, our strength and our hope. I love you, Rob, to the moon and back and then some!

To my precious, darling kids -- you will never know how much you mean to me. You guys have bumped along with us, and have endured so much in your young lives. I am grateful for your love, understanding and willingness to work through the barriers that keep us from our best and from God. I know that all of this has not been easy, for any of you. You all have had your own struggles, and, out of it all, God has granted us more strength as a family. Through the years, I have admired the relationship you three have had together -- to watch you grow and be, not only siblings to one another, but friends too. Alex, Corinne and Rebekah, you have taught me to have fun, how to be a kid and how to love and nurture another human being. For this, I thank you. I love you guys to the moon and back and then some.

And to my mom; without her support, this would not be possible right now. *Mom, we've been "through the ringer" and our relationship has come out stronger than I thought possible. Thank you. I love you.*

To my dad, for always keeping the door of faith open for me. *I am forever grateful to you for this. I love you.*

To my siblings; *we've journey through our family life together. We've had some good laughs and good times. Thank you for being part of my journey. Love you both!*

A very special "thank you" goes to my best friend Delia, who has been my spiritual sidekick for over nine years. For pushing this project forward and "starting the way" to get it going. *Your strength, support and belief in my book, and me, have given me great courage to move forward. I love you with all my heart you crazy girl!*

To all my friends in my bible study group who have given so much support through the completion of this book.

To my abusers; *you know who you are. I pray for you. I, in some strange way, thank you for your part in this. For what I have received through it all is far greater than I could ever imagine. I know the love of God and the freedom that comes with forgiveness. I forgive you both and I pray you receive the grace and peace that only God can give.*

Preface

Hi! My name is Christina. Chris, or Chrissy, for short. Actually, I just recently started using my full name; for as long I could remember it was always Chrissy. Not that any of that matters.

If you've picked up this book, I'm assuming there's some bumps and hurdles in your life that you may be facing. I urge you to please continue reading on through these next pages. If there's just one piece of advice, or something that takes hold of your heart as you read this story, I will feel as if I have reached my goal.

Through my own experiences and challenges, I have often wondered, *Why is this happening?* And as I sit here and write this, I fully accept and understand why I endured the situations that I encountered in my life.

A few years back, when I started writing to "reach out" to others, my life was hitting a terrible low. My kids were getting older and a lot more independent, and I realized they still needed me (but for different reasons). Two of them were in high school, and the youngest attended junior high. I sat wallowing in pity, thinking, *Oh my goodness, what am I going to do with myself now?* I sat there and prayed. I asked the Lord to plant an idea in my heart. I asked Him, *What do you want from me now, Lord?*

Out of "the blue," I heard this voice in my head: "Write a book. You've had enough experiences in life -- some good, some bad, some dreadful -- and now you can use them to reach out to others." That is when I felt my spirits lift, and I was determined to do something for others. My life experiences were going to help others in some way.

Now, I pause briefly and take in the beautiful day that God has given to me. The sun is shining so brightly this morning, and the air is crisp and cool.

I am able to count my blessings everyday and be grateful for all that I have. It is truly a blessing that I woke-up this morning; that I was able to take my youngest daughter to school, and that I was able to walk my dog. I am blessed that I made it home safely. All the small things, that seem so "every day," are blessings. You may not be in that receptive attitude at this moment, but you *can* learn to be. You *can* learn to see the small things as gifts from above.

I don't know what you are facing at this time in your life, but I can assure you that there is a light at the end of the tunnel. I know how hard it is to keep your eyes on the light when the rest of your world seems to be caving in around you. There will always be obstacles and challenges in our lives. We endure them, and, by doing so, we become stronger and better people if we choose to *respond* to life instead of *react* to it. Reacting to negative situations doesn't change what's happening, and often magnifies it. By choosing a proactive approach and taking one day at a time, one step at a time, we are able to cope and positively respond.

It wasn't always this way for me. I had to learn the very hard way in life to get to where I am today, and to be in the frame of mind I'm able to be in through challenges. I continually encountered the same situations, negatively reacting the same way and hoping for a change. It wasn't until I made the change to positively respond to those situations that my life started to take a different turn.

So, let's go. Come with me through the pages of this book, through the pages of my life.

April, 1992

Oh no, no, no, no, no! It can't be! I thought as I stood there in the high school hallway listening to the doctor's voice on the other line of the telephone.

"Positive." he said. "Please come in and see me."

Oh, dear God. What have I done? What will I do? This can't be happening. So many thoughts were going through my mind. As I hung up, my heart raced; I felt lightheaded. I was only sixteen years old. How could this have happened? Well, I knew exactly how this had happened. The decisions and choices that lay ahead of me were just overwhelming. My first thought was that I would run away, but that idea, as good as I thought it sounded, was crazy. Where on earth would I go? Where would *we* go? This was an example of allowing the situation to determine where I was going in my life. At that very moment, as I questioned myself, I had already made a choice and a decision: I was keeping this baby.

> *... I have good plans for you, not plans to hurt you. I will give you hope and a good future* (Jer. 29:11 New Century Version).

And so, my journey of uncertainties, decisions and challenges had begun. There was no question, or even a thought, about not keeping this baby. There was a life inside me; a small heart was beating as I stood there replaying my conversation with the doctor in my head.

"Yes, Christina, you are pregnant," he told me sympathetically. I couldn't explain how I was feeling, and I was too numb to cry.

A million things ran through my mind, and I felt like I was going to faint. I thought about my parents and my family. I wondered how on earth I was going to tell them about this.

I pictured myself saying, "Hey, Mom and Dad. You know, I just turned sixteen and guess what, I'm pregnant." *No, that is not going to work,* I thought. All my life, I never felt like I could confide or talk to my parents about anything personal. It was sad to say, but we never nurtured a relationship like that. Personal issues like boys, sex and self-esteem were unapproachable in our household.

As far as I could remember, there was never any sitting around with my parents and siblings to just talk about our days or whatever was going on in our lives. It didn't happen, ever. However, there were a lot of issues happening in my family. There were a lot of secrets, and Mom and Dad did not communicate openly about themselves, let alone family issues.

I felt Dad was a very quiet, unapproachable man. I always felt very awkward around him. Many times I did have the feeling to want to talk to Dad and tell him what was going on in our family, but I was told to make sure I never did or else he would have a heart attack and die. Well, that was not something I wanted on my conscience!

Growing up, there was much anger and rage in the family. So much yelling, loudness, and hysterical fits. I thought I was the cause of all this madness. There was something wrong with me, I reasoned. I recall my parent's relationship as cold, lifeless and emotionless, except for the anger. It seemed as if there were two families in one. The first family was when Dad was at work. When he was, the crazy insanity happened. Money was stolen, alcohol was replaced with water, and jewellery went missing. Mom would scream and yell and lash out at God.

I couldn't understand (at my age) what was really going on, but, for some strange, crazy reason, I felt I was to blame. As years of this insanity continued, I realized there were many problems in this family, and things were just not right.

3

And then there was the other side of the family: the one people would see. My parents would put on their "happy faces" in front of business partners or colleagues, and go about their fraudulent lives. But behind closed doors, it was a different story. I was often left home on weekends with my siblings, an older brother and sister, to care for me. Though that was the plan, they both had other intentions. My sister would go away to be with her boyfriend, and my brother would take this opportunity to have his "friends" over. I thought it was cool to be at a party with my brother's friends. And what a party indeed! There would be a lot of drugs and drinking at these parties. I was left unattended, often sitting outside on the front porch until four in the morning. I saw the drugs, the girls, the nastiness of what drugs, drinking and irresponsibility caused, and what followed. As I think back, I recall the anger welling up inside me, feeling hopeless and helpless to what was happening. Who could I tell? I had always hated drugs. One evening, when I was eleven or twelve, two family members were smoking marijuana on the back porch. I became enraged and opened the door to tell them to stop. They called me names, told me to shut up and go back inside, and said that it was nothing. I felt so angry and stupid. I felt the hatred towards them, to the drugs and to my whole self and my life, grow stronger and stronger. I tried to tell my mother what was happening after many weekends of the same craziness, but it was to no avail.

Nothing was ever done. My Dad had no clue either. This lifestyle of our family continued like this for many years.

Along with all this baggage, I had another issue to deal with on my own: a horrific and terrible situation. For many years, two different family members sexually abused me. This abuse started when I was three years old. Sadly, our families got together very often. Every weekend, we would either be at their place or they would be at our home. These two family members, at different opportunities, would force me away to a private place and invade my body in ways that are unspeakable. As I remember these days, I cringe and feel great pain. I was alone; I was helpless in defending myself against these attacks. Week after week, year after year, abuse after abuse, my spirit was broken down, destroyed and lost. My childhood was robbed from me with the very first attack. As each day passed, I hated myself more and more.

During the ongoing sexual abuse, I was ashamed and felt dirty. *Why is this happening to me?* I would often ask myself; but the only answer I would get was that I was awful and that I deserved it. I often wondered why that was, and I questioned why I thought I deserved to be abused in such a manner. Year after year, the torture continued and I silently suffered. I became bitter and angry. Not only did I despise myself, but I hated everyone around me. I resented my parents for not knowing this was happening to me, and for not rescuing me and saving me from the agony that plagued me so many hours of my young life. This abuse has reeked destruction in my life and in the relationships that I have had. The effects that this abuse has scarred me with are many. My innocence was stolen from me. Growing up, I was unable to play with any of my dolls. I tried, but it soon led to a rage and hate bubbling within me that I would end up beating and destroying them. The abuse would then turn on myself. I remember being a little girl, of around five or six, and beating my own body; punching myself and hitting myself because of the anger I felt towards what was happening to me. I was angry that no one was helping me; I was angry no one knew. My goodness, if I could go back to that little girl, I would hold her, hug her and protect her. I would comfort her and bring her to safety.

After several years, the torment suddenly stopped. I don't know exactly when, but my abusers eventually left me alone. My spirit, or what was left of it, felt (to me) like it couldn't be fixed. The degrading encounters were placed in a file way back in my mind and I never spoke of it, ever. As time went on, how I felt about myself continued to worsen. I didn't think it was possible for someone to hate themselves as much as I did. I was convinced no one could ever love the monster I felt that I was.

The thought of taking my own life crossed my mind several

times, and was attempted on two occasions. Thankfully, I was not successful.

I became very withdrawn from my family. I did not want to talk to anyone. I wanted to be left alone. The incredible anger and rage that bubbled up inside me was uncontrollable. I lashed out at home, fought with my siblings, and destroyed the house. My education went downhill. I couldn't be bothered with school or trying to make anything of myself because I felt unworthy to be successful in any way. I kept telling myself, *I'm good for nothing except one thing, and that is for people to take advantage of me.*

I hated life with a passion and wondered why God was allowing mine to continue. With the life I was leading, it was so hard for me to understand how there even was a God and why He was doing this to me. Anywhere I could find a place to put the blame, I did. It was everybody else's fault my life was so miserable and shameful. During those years, my parents had their own issues to deal with, and, deep down, I felt responsible for their unhappiness with each other. I often condemned myself for things that happened in my external world that I had no control of. My mere existence caused disorder and misery to others. I had absolutely no use for myself or anyone. Or so I believed.

So here I was, pregnant at the fresh age of sixteen. At times, I wished that I was stuck in a nightmare; but no, this was reality. Once again, I blamed God for doing this to me. Yes, it was His fault I was in this situation. *What am I going to do?* I asked myself. I can't explain what happened at that precise moment, but I made a decision: I was going to be the best Mom that I could be. I decided that I was going to do everything differently from my family. This baby was going to have everything I didn't have, and the abuse I suffered was not going to be part of his, or her, young life. I had no clue how this was going to happen, or not happen. I just told myself it would be different.

That decision temporarily lifted my spirits, but I still had to tell my family.

I was quickly brought back down to earth with the thought of telling my parents. Given our very difficult relationship, I could barely speak to them about day to day stuff -- how on God's green earth was I going to tell them I was pregnant?

Two months went by since I had found out, and with that came morning sickness that lasted twenty-four hours a day. Food disgusted me, and the smell of coffee brewing in the early morning twisted my insides. Trying to hide how I was feeling was getting harder and harder. I was so weak and tired. I was unable to eat a single thing; I couldn't even keep water down. Over the next few months, I lost a lot of weight. I could barely stand.

I was still attending school at this time; so, I would get up as usual and, when no one was looking, take a handful of my dad's vitamins and head out the door. By the time I would get to school I would be so violently ill that I would never made it to class. A very good friend of mine at the time was supportive to me. I filled her in on what was going on, and she did all that she could to help me. She offered advice and found some information about a teenage pregnancy place where girls could go for help. I made an appointment and she came with me to check out the place. It was a beautiful centre that housed teenagers. They gave them a room and offered many programs. At first I had decided, *Yes, I'm moving in here!* Again, the thought of running away had popped up; however, I now had a place to go. But something inside me didn't feel right. Here I was, making decisions and plans while my parents and family still had no idea of what was happening.

Little did I know, my mother was very suspicious of what was occurring. She was doing her own research, and was putting two and two together. I had written a letter to my cousin in which I confided to her my problem. She wrote back telling me she was glad I decided to keep the baby and not have an abortion. I kept the letter in my backpack. My "detective" mother went through my bag and read the letter. I can't even begin to imagine what she must have felt reading those words. Mom went one step further to confirm what she read and called the doctor who, in turn, gave her the answer she needed.

One Saturday morning I couldn't get out of bed, and my mother came into my bedroom and sat down. She said she wanted to talk to me. I was praying to God for her to leave because I was about to throw-up. Needless to say, she stayed. Mom came right out and asked me, "Are you pregnant?" Shocked with her question, I told her I wasn't. She asked me again. I said, "What are you talking about Mom? I'm not." My mother informed me that she had called the doctor the day before and he told her I was. I was speechless. What could I say? I could no longer delay the inevitable. I put my face in my pillow, ashamed, and cried. Surprisingly, my mom took the news calmly. I guess she had had the previous day to deal with her feelings (whatever they were). I felt relieved. Oddly, part of me felt like the weight of the world was lifted off of me, another part of me felt so upset that the doctor told my mother, and a whole other part of me was glad that I did not have to break the news myself.

My dad was away on a business trip at this time. Mom said she was going to tell him when he got back. My mother didn't even ask me what I was going to decide, it was like she already knew that my decision was to keep the baby. Late one Sunday night, my dad came home. I remember I was in my sister's bedroom while my poor mother carried out the burden of telling Dad that his youngest child was pregnant at the age of sixteen. I didn't know what to expect, since Mom took the news quite easily. How was this going to go? As I was lost in thought, I heard my dad yell, "Kick her out of the house!"

My heart broke, and I thought my previous idea of running away wasn't such a bad one. The thought of my dad coming upstairs to "give me a licking" crossed my mind, so I quickly went to hide under my sister's bed (though my dad never laid a hand on me growing up). I got halfway under and realized I didn't fit. Why didn't I fit? As the months went on, I failed to notice my boobs had grown! So there I was, half way under the bed with the fear that my dad was going to kill me.

My dad refused to speak to me for the entire week. It was a long, challenging week. If there had been another place for me to go, I would have gone. The uneasiness and tension in the family, and in our home, was so thick. I pretty much kept to myself and remained alone in my bedroom (coming out only to eat and throw-up). If I had been feeling better, it would have been easier to deal with what was happening. I was so nauseated and fatigued that I could not think straight. I mostly ate crackers, and drank chamomile tea and grape juice. The cravings for certain foods were overwhelming. My mom did her best to get me the foods I wanted, but after I ate I would spend the next two hours hugging the toilet. I became so weak that I could barely stand. At this point, the way I was feeling made me uncertain about whether or not I was going to live. I slept most of the time, and can't even remember thinking about anything or even caring about what was going to happen. Physically, emotionally and mentally, I felt that I just could not deal with this problem.

One day I was cleaning up my room when my dad knocked on the door. He came in and, without judgment or scolding, asked me one question, "Do you want this baby?" I answered that I did. He said, "Okay then," gave me a hug and walked out of my room without another word. That was his acceptance of the situation.

It all started to hit me. I sat on my bed and cried. I didn't fully realize, nor could I comprehend at the time, the heartache my parents felt. The shame I felt was no match for the embarrassment and upset my parents were going through. How were they going to face their family and friends? Here I was just thinking of myself, while, in reality, they were going to have to do the dirty work in exposing what an irresponsible teenager they had. My parents knew a lot of people; they travelled very often around the US, growing their business. Our home had revolving doors -- people were always coming and going. Unless my parents secretly decided to ship me away to a convent, or lock me up for nine months in the attic, my condition was eventually going to be noticed.

But that wasn't the plan at all. If they felt shame, which I believe they did, they didn't show it. As the days and weeks went on, I suddenly realized that my parents were in this with me for the long haul.

I had dropped out of high school when I was in my third year. It was awful because I had a month and a half left to go. However, I was partially glad to be rid of school because I was never really good at it anyways, and I thought this was what I was supposed to do; this is what happened to teenagers who got pregnant. My mentality at this time was reacting to the situation and going with what I felt society deemed appropriate for teenage moms.

So here I was, a pregnant high school dropout, not knowing where my life was going or where I would end up. What I did know was that I was pregnant -- I was having a baby. I was having a baby! "Dear God," I said over and over again. It baffled my mind. I had no job, no money and I never really thought about *how* I was going to take care of this baby. Was clothing, food and diapers just going to fall out of the sky? Now I was faced with the reality of these challenges. With my pessimistic outlook on life, I wallowed in self-pity and disgrace about what I had done. I was going to be just another statistic.

Where was my baby's father in all of this? "Dad," whom we shall refer to as Geo, was too busy hiding from his parents.

You see, I was not too popular with his parents because of my nationality. While I was going through my own hell, he said nothing at all to his family. I was four months pregnant and his family knew nothing. I didn't know if he thought that this situation would just disappear, or if he had no intention of sticking around.

Geo and I were very good friends before we started seeing each other romantically (in the fall of 1990). One thing led to another, and our young relationship grew. We were both fourteen years old and went to the same high school when we met. About a year after we started dating, I had met his family. For the most part, they were pleasant. His mom realized we had been together for some time, and she made it known that she did not approve. She preferred her children to date within their own heritage, and I wasn't part of that. Hence, they rejected me.

One day, my mom had asked me if Geo's parents knew, and I came out and told her, "No, they don't." When I proceeded to tell her why, Mom was appalled. She had me call him to find out if his mom was home, and off the two of us went to meet with her. The nerves that attacked my stomach were outrageous; I started to hyperventilate. My mom was on a mission, and she was out to give his mother a piece of her mind. Thinking back, my mom, no matter what she was going through or how she was dealing with the situation, was there for me.

We arrived at their home. Geo's mom invited us in, and we had coffee (actually, my mother had coffee as I had stopped drinking it when I found out that I was pregnant). Thankfully, my mother broke the ice and started to speak. Mom went on to speak about how Geo and I had been dating for some time now, and had unfortunately gotten ourselves in trouble. I highly doubt his mom was expecting to hear that she was going to be a grandmother. My mother told her the news. I wanted to crawl in a hole and hide. I realized that no parent takes this news easily, and his mother freaked. First, she did not believe that it was Geo's baby, and then she went on to blame me and claim that it was my entire fault. That is when my mother lost it. She firmly and sternly told her it was both of our faults. Not one person over the other was to blame. After a short silence, we got up, left, and, with not one nice word to say about Geo's mother, walked home.

I didn't speak to Geo for a few days. The stress was overtaking me, and everything seemed like a blur. The utter exhaustion was too much to bear. I spent the next few days in bed, trying to hide away, slipping into deep sleeps, hoping and praying that all of this would be gone when I awoke. But, as some of us may know, no matter where and how we may try to hide or run away, there is no *true* escaping what is happening.

My baby's father came to see me, and we sat on the porch and talked for hours. I'm sure he was dealing with his own horror. His parents wanted nothing, absolutely nothing, to do with me or with this baby. They were willing to pay him $25,000 to convince me to get an abortion. I was mortified. I was almost five months pregnant; a baby was living inside me, a baby whose heart was beating. And they wanted me to destroy that? Never! Geo didn't approve of that idea either. He told me he informed his parents that he would not do it.

I can't even begin to describe how I was feeling. Physically, I was drained. The pregnancy was really taking a toll on my body. By this stage, I had lost almost twenty pounds and I was very weak. Emotionally, I couldn't even feel anything anymore. I didn't care if Geo stuck around or not. All I knew was that I had no more tears to cry at this point. There was nothing left inside me.

As the weeks went on, we stayed together. It eventually seemed to me that I was growing (in more ways than one) and that Geo was the ball and chain that I was dragging along. I was busy preparing for our baby, making lists, going to the doctor's appointments, and dealing with the changes of my sixteen-year-old body. Everywhere I went, people stared at me.

I felt that I had to deal with the gossip and stares while Geo went along on his merry way. From what I had seen, life didn't change much for him (though this may have been just my perception of the situation). Thinking back, it must have been difficult for Geo to live in a household with parents who didn't support or reassure him that everything was going to be OK. At one point, I remember he said that he didn't care anymore about what his parents were saying. He fought with them, particularly his mother, all the time. And contrary to his parent' wishes, Geo and I continued to see each other. The way I saw it, I believed that his father would have eventually "come around" if his mother had "allowed" him to. But his family had established a tradition of "sticking to their own kind." I'm sure that they felt humiliated, ashamed and embarrassed of the situation, and that they were unable to support their own son in it. Their concern was more with what their friends and family would say, so they chose to have nothing at all to do with the whole issue.

However, as the days passed, Geo and I started fighting over all sorts of things, especially the fact that he carried on going to clubs and parties while I stayed home. It was then I realized that the pregnancy, and the reality of becoming a parent, had not affected him yet. I didn't know what I was in for yet either, but I started to get used to the idea that life was about to change for me, and everyone around me.

As the months passed, I headed into my third trimester of pregnancy. I loved this baby despite all the nonsense that had continued on. I felt alive, as if I finally had a purpose in life. I loved when I felt this human being moving inside me. I felt connected to this baby, and I didn't even know him, or her, yet. I would secretly read to my baby and talk to him/her. I would tell my baby how much I loved him/her, how I was going to love and take care of him/her to the best of my ability. However, this was all done secretly due to the shame and disgrace I felt for showing affection towards another. The sexual abuse that I had encountered distorted my views on affection and love. As long as I was alone with my baby, I could fully love him/her without feeling judged or shamed.

December 25, 1992

My due date was just a couple of days away. It was Christmas day, and I was due December 27. I remember waking up that morning and thinking that next year, at this time, it would be my baby's first Christmas. I smiled to myself. My family and I got dressed and took pictures. I remember I took a picture with my sister in front of our Christmas tree, and I looked hilarious! Here I was, skinny as a rail, with a big belly that looked ready to explode. I had broken blood vessels on my pale face (with my hair pulled back), and had bangs that were clearly cut too short. I can laugh at that photo of myself now, but it was not so funny back then. We spent Christmas Day at my Grandma's house. It was great: my two best cousins were there, and we talked and joked around trying to be just like old times. But all of us knew that it was not "just like old times." They supported me very much, and promised to be there for me the best they could. When it was time to leave, we hugged each other and realized that, the next time they saw me, I would be a mother. I turned to walk away, and got into the car. I was scared. My due date was two days away, and nothing was going to stop this baby from coming. As things with Geo and his parents were still not right, I realized that my baby's father still had so much growing up to do. We drove home, and I went straight to bed.

December 27, 1992

Three weeks after turning seventeen, I went into labour.

It was a bright, sunny, cold day. I put my slippers on, and went downstairs to eat breakfast. I sat with my mother and sister. We talked and spent time together. It was peaceful and relaxing. I remember feeling I had to go to the bathroom. I went upstairs, did my business and then realized, *Oh my God, I'm in full-blown labor.* I called my mom, and she said very calmly, "All right, it's time. Let's get ready to go to the hospital."

I was excited and very scared. I debated calling my baby's father. I wasn't allowed to call his house, so I hesitated. To make a long story short, I got the nerve to call. Shaking, I dialed his number, praying he would answer. Unfortunately, his lovely mother answered. I asked to speak to him, but she told me no. I said OK, and asked her if she could please tell him that I had gone into labor and I would be at the hospital. She started to yell and scream at me over the phone about how we were too young to be having a baby and how stupid I was. Did she not know that I knew we were too young for this? Of course I knew! It was not my plan to get pregnant at sixteen! But that is what happened, and I was not going to destroy a life because of my irresponsibility. I was this baby's mother, no matter what. I didn't know how I was going to manage, but I just knew that somehow I would.

My aunt drove us to the hospital. She and her family lived down the street from us while all this was happening. I was so glad that my mom had her for support throughout this ordeal. As far as I knew, my aunt had not judged me nor said anything bad to anyone about me or my family. She and my cousins would come to visit almost every day, and they showed excitement and happiness for me (despite my age). We would joke and laugh, and they always looked on the bright side of life and my situation. They looked forward to the birth of this child.

When we arrived at the hospital, I was quickly admitted and taken up to the Labor and Delivery unit. I was filled with all sorts of emotions: fear, panic, excitement, and so many other feelings were running through me. Did I mention pain? Yes, the pain came on very quickly. Geo did eventually arrive at the hospital. He was not impressed or happy that male doctors were "looking" at me and helping me through the birth. I recall a time when, as I was pushing, he whispered in my ear something to the effect of "getting me back" for allowing male doctors to assist me. I was not impressed about male doctors looking at me either! The effects of my abuse had made me feel very self-conscious, and seeing doctors was out of the question for me. I gave any male doctor a very hard time to examine me. In this situation of giving birth, I had very little choice. My female doctor was away on vacation. At that moment, I had wished that Geo was not in the room with me. I had such mixed emotions, and the incredible shame that overcame me was horrendous.

To make a long labor story short, I was a trooper and used no pain medication. Several strenuous hours later (eighteen to be exact), my six pound two ounce, 21.5 inch long son entered this world. One look in those big brown eyes, and everything I had encountered over the past nine months seemed to evaporate in the enormous feeling of love that instantly overtook me. This precious boy was surrounded by so much love. My family was all around to welcome him into this world.

I remained in the hospital for three days. Lack of sleep followed, and the endless efforts to nurse my new son were draining. During quiet moments, I looked at this baby that I considered a precious gift. He was so tiny and perfect. Looking after him came naturally to me, and I felt that this was what I was born to do. I felt alive and filled with purpose.

A situation that was causing so much turmoil and conflict had put a sense of peace, love and life in my heart and soul. I don't even think I remembered thanking God for this precious gift. He was the One I blamed for all the craziness and pain in my life, and now I was at a place of peace. How could that be?

The day came when it was time to leave the hospital. I was excited to go home to love and care for my new baby. I bundled-up my baby against the winter chill, and we went home. I could not have known what lay ahead. Being a full-time mom, while living at home with my parents and siblings, proved to be very challenging. My sister, who is four and a half years older than me, was attending college, and was finishing her Early Childhood Education studies. She offered a lot of advice on how to care for my son; advice on how to "properly" talk to him and teach him. I did my best to take it all in. I started to feel that my sister probably knew what to do better than I did since she was in school. I would spend time with my son; love him, feed him and nurture our relationship. But this was very difficult at times because I felt like I was being watched and graded on my ability to be his mother.

I know my family meant well, but there was always some sort of criticism on how I was handling my baby (and motherhood in general). I knew that I was so fortunate to have so much help. Mom provided so many material things I needed for my son -- she bought him food, clothing and so much more. Although I was very thankful, there was this ugly, gnawing feeling inside of me. As the days and months passed, my feelings of self-hatred started to grow and bubble up again. I started to feel that I was no good, and that I was causing harm to my child. I was often told not to do things my way; I wasn't right, their way was better and correct. I was told how to read books to my child and how to put him to sleep. If I showed any frustration, my mother took my son and simply did things her way. As that continued, my son seemed to start to prefer being with my mother instead of me. The bond that he and I had shared together seemed to be weakening. I started to feel useless, and felt that my son did not need me. I felt ashamed and like I was not a good mother. I felt like a failure.

It was around this time that I started to abuse myself in order to ease my pain. I started deliberately missing meals. I limited my food intake to once, maybe twice, a day. As I started to master and discipline myself with the one or two daily meals, I started to skip days altogether. If I was weak, I ate something on my "no food" days; for appropriate punishment, I did not eat for the next three days. I also added plenty of vigorous exercise to this insane lifestyle (that I had initially started in order to ease my pain and anguish).

This cycle of self-abuse continued day after day. It became something that I could do well, and I poured all of my energy and self into it. It became the first thing I thought about every morning when I woke-up. As I starved myself hour after agonizing hour, I would tell myself that I needed to be thinner and look better so that I would be more fit for my family and child. I put all my focus on this deprivation. I felt that I needed to look different, be different, and change my appearance in order to be loved and accepted by my family. With each pound lost, nothing changed. There was still fighting and arguing in the family, and by now I had officially ended the relationship with Geo.

Out of anger and frustration and hurt, I refused my son's father any visitation. This was my child -- I was the one who had done, and was still doing, all the hard work -- and I felt that he had no "right" to see him. Out of my selfishness and pain, I lashed out. Today, I have a very hard time forgiving myself for this action. I severed a bond that could have grown between my son and his father. Because I was hurting, I reacted badly and hurt others. The time lost between my son and his father can never be replaced. At the time, I could not be compassionate to Geo because I was so self-absorbed in my own hurt and pain. I felt that I had, and deserved, control. I decided that if I hurt and pushed people away, they could not hurt me again.

I lied to my son over the years, and I held this secret so close inside me. Many people knew of this; I made sure they knew what I was doing. This secret, the identity of my baby's father, I planned to take to the grave with me. That was my plan. However, in December 2009, I learned that my secret had been revealed at my children's elementary school. I was mortified. What was I to do? I prayed long and hard. I prayed for guidance, I prayed for courage and I prayed for the strength to finally release this secret. My son was in grade twelve, his last year of high school. How could I destroy his life now?

My son, Alex. Makes me grin as I think of what an amazing young man God has created him to be. My gift from God. We call him Al or, my personal, little name for him, Buster. God has blessed this boy with a good heart open to accepting the Lord in his life. Alex and I eventually grew our relationship and mended the broken pieces. A lot of this healing needed to come from me. I put much time and effort into nurturing this relationship, and the payoff has been beautiful. Alex and I would play together, pray together and learn from one another.

Many people thought of him as a troubled child who was going to cause me many problems. I never believed that, not for one instant. When Alex started school, there was something special about him. Even before he started school, I would sit with him and teach him the alphabet, his numbers and how to write his name. He soaked this up and easily grasped all that I taught him. His little brain grew in wisdom and knowledge. He went into school ahead of the game.

At one point, the school suggested that he skip a grade, but we felt it would have put unnecessary pressure on him (especially since he was already one of the youngest children in his grade due to his December birthday). Alex continued in school, excelling in all areas. When he did something, he did his best.

He and I are blessed to have open communication. He tells me many things. He demonstrates trust in me. And because I also demonstrate trustworthiness in him, I am a safe place to share. With this closeness, we are able to share appropriately on personal issues with ourselves, and others, if there is an issue within the family.

Alex's life led him to journey with God. Through his choices and the way the road went, he ended up at a University that led him to a Christian organization. Through this organization, Alex has had the opportunity to serve alongside Christ in another country across the world. How this child defeated the odds that were against him leaves me in awe. I am truly inspired seeing how God moved in and made his life wonderful. He was not going to be another statistic.

So, one day in December, I decided to let him in on my burden. I wondered how I was going to share with Alex about his biological father. I won't lie, I was petrified. I expected him to be angry, and for him to cut me out of his life. I expected him to run out of our home to distance himself from me. Guilt, shame and a feeling of unworthiness came like a tsunami flooding my heart. In my mind, I was preparing to lose him again. I knew it was time for the story of his birth to come out in the open. I felt like I was forced to tell him. The secret was hitting too close to home. I prayed. I sent Alex a text message while he was at school telling him I needed to speak to him about something important. I sent the text so that I would be able to go through with telling him.

He came home from school that evening. God is a funny Guy, and works in mysterious ways. Both of my daughters were at friends' houses and my husband was working late. I feel that God arranged it so that we could be alone together. It was just Alex and I. My hands were shaking. We sat on the couch across from each other. I told him I needed to tell him about something, about when he was a baby. I proceeded to tell him the whole story. As I spoke, it occurred to me that I was sharing the story from a victim's perspective. Was this maybe out of fear of losing him? Or maybe from not really being honest at the time about my part in the whole situation? Whatever it was, that was the way it went and the story came out. I waited for Alex to say or do something. I half expected him to lash out and run out the door.

Then he spoke. He said, "Mom, don't worry about it. Look at what we have, and look at how far we've come". I just about passed out at his response! *Who was this guy?* My jaw dropped -- I was stunned. He then admitted that, deep down in his heart, he knew he had a biological dad somewhere. I asked him why he didn't say or ask about it, and he said that he felt he didn't need to. He then went on to share that he considered Dad (his current father) as his real dad. And he also said that knowing the truth made him love and respect his present father even more for raising him with love. My heart melted. I got on my knees and thanked God for His work in our lives. This could not have been better orchestrated by anyone else than He who works all things out for our good.

However, living at home with Alex as a baby was emotionally, mentally and spiritually difficult. I felt like I was a burden on my family. My siblings and I fought constantly, and I was often blamed for causing the fights and arguments. I was not happy, and my life was falling apart. I lost all my friends, and I lost my boyfriend. I even lost my own child to my mother (who gladly took over the role). I was full of anger, hatred, resentment and hostility to others, but I mostly directed this hostility towards myself. The turmoil within me ate whatever emotions or feelings I had left. I once again lashed out at God for this horrible, loveless life that He had given me.

A couple of months prior to my eighteenth birthday, in October 1993, one of my only friends at the time came to visit. She was just coming out of a relationship, as I was just coming out of the breakup from my baby's father; and there we were, two broken hearted teenagers. We got this crazy idea to put personal ads in the newspaper for fun. These ads would be designed to help us find a slew of potential "significant others" who would express loving interest in us. We laughed and giggled and cried, and had a great night reminiscing about our high school days. Having agreed to put two ads in the local paper, we began looking for dates. As the ad ran in the paper for a month, we checked our messages to see if anyone responded. The replies came flooding in.

It was quite comical reading and listening to the replies to our personal ads. One particular reply I received seemed to tug at my heart, although there was nothing different or spectacular about it. My friend and I listened to this reply, and actually made fun of how this person sounded over the answering machine message. We listened to it over and over again, and laughed our heads off. I didn't keep this guy's phone number, and I deleted all the replies I received. And life went on. But over the next few days, this guy's voice kept replaying in my head. I was unable to forget his number. I wrote his number down on a scrap paper, put it in my drawer, and gave it no more thought.

December 4, 1993.

My eighteenth birthday. I always hated my birthdays. I felt this was not a day to celebrate. I felt and believed that I was a curse to my family and eleven-month-old son. I recall how dead, unhappy and so alone I felt. Here I was, celebrating my eighteenth birthday with my parents and two of their older friends. Could this be what life was? Is this where my life was going? I was trying to celebrate my eighteenth birthday, all the while feeling horrible inside. I was sad, lonely, and depressed, carrying a heavy self-loathing that bubbled up from the depths of my insides.

I remember leaving the dinner table and going up to my room. I started rummaging around in my drawer and finding the phone number I had previously written down of the guy who had called in response to my ad. His name is Rob, I thought to myself, *What do I have to lose?* With shaking hands, I called the number. The answering machine picked up, and there was a woman's voice on the other end. I thought briefly to myself, *What kind of jerk is this?* However, my misgivings did not stop me from leaving my own message.

During my younger years, and because of my childhood sexual abuse, I was very shy and afraid of speaking to people (especially over the phone). It was very difficult for me to order pizza over the phone, or to even go into a store and buy my bus tickets. I found it very difficult to make any decisions for myself, and, not surprisingly, I had no clue what my likes and dislikes were. I would hide myself from the world, and think of myself as a coward. It was not easy for me to leave a message on the phone the night that I called Rob.

After making the call and leaving my message, I went back to join the "party". I felt like I was there in body, but my mind and spirit were else where. The rest of that evening is a blur. A few hours later, a phone call came in. *It was him!* I answered. I was so nervous, yet excited at the same time! We talked about random subjects for about ten minutes on the phone, and I remember thinking, *Wow, he sounds so cute!* He asked if I wanted to meet him for coffee that very night, and I was on cloud nine! He wanted to meet me right away. I wanted to drop everything and just run out the door. But I didn't. I explained to him that it was my birthday and that I had guests over. He said, "Oh, Happy birthday," and we made arrangements to speak to each other the following day. With that little encounter, my heart was filled with happiness. I was so thrilled, and I felt like someone was actually interested in speaking to me. To *me*! I went to bed that night with an ear-to-ear grin.

Rob and I started talking on the phone every day. I made it perfectly clear during one of our early talks that I had a young son. I wanted to be right upfront about that. His response was, "cool." I was flying high! Here I was, speaking to a guy that I hadn't met yet, and he was already accepting and OK with the fact that I had a child.

Could this get any better? I asked myself. Rob and I would speak with each other for hours and hours (thank goodness for cordless phones). As days passed, I realized that I felt happy, and that there was a new burst of excitement and life flowing through me. Rob would talk with me and listen to me, which seemed like something out of a movie. I was giddy; I was unable to sleep most nights. A week went by, and we spoke several times a day (and some nights until four or five in the morning). I recall saying to my friend, "I have a feeling I'm going to marry this guy," even though I hadn't even met him yet. Later that week, he invited me to accompany him to his brother's Christmas party. We planned for him to meet me at the subway station by my house at 4:30pm Saturday evening. It appears that the month of December had become the "happening" month for me.

Rob had moved to Toronto in October of 1993 from

Edmonton, Alberta. He moved in with his brother and sister-in-law (the woman on the answering machine) at the same time I was putting my dating ad in the paper. Thinking back to that God-incidence (not to be confused with "coincidence"), I'm still blown away at the way God orchestrated this union.

I think back to that Saturday, December 11th, when Rob and I would finally meet, and I remember how giddy and excited my friend and I were. Talking to her on the phone, she told me that that same night she was also going on a date with someone she had met from our personal ads! I remember sharing with her that I felt deep down inside that Rob was the one -- he was the one I was waiting for. It seemed like my knight in shining armour had finally come to rescue me from this awful wretched life I was living.

I was at the subway station at 4:15 in the evening. I hid behind a wall and peeked out to watch the men that walked by. There was this one young guy who was hanging around, and I remember praying, *God, please don't let that be him.* I was actually thinking at that point that I could always get back on the bus and go home.

Through all these feelings that he was the one, and that he was going to fix my life and love me, I felt very shallow and angry at myself for entertaining the idea of going back home because I wasn't physically attracted to this guy. To my relief, the young man walked away. It was not him.

I decided to walk around the station. No one was there. I started to get very discouraged. I walked down a long hallway, and, at the end of it, I saw this blond, very good looking guy walking with a rose in his hand. I started praying, *Please God, please God, let that be him.* As we got closer, he was looking at me, and I was looking at him. He was the first one to speak, and he said "Chris?" I said, "Yes," and my heart melted. He hugged me and kissed me on the cheek. The butterflies in my tummy were fluttering so bad I almost threw-up!

We got on the subway to go to his brother's place, which was in Ajax (about an hour and a half trip with the Go train and buses). It was a twenty minute walk from the Go station to his brother's house, and it was a freezing cold, bitter windy night. I remember it was about minus twenty-five degrees. We made small talk on the trip. Now I was really nervous; there was no phone to hide behind for safety. I was here in the flesh, and so was he. I wondered if he liked the way I looked. I wondered if he still wanted me to go to the party. All these crazy questions flooded my mind and took me away from being in the moment.

We finally arrived at his brother's place. I was frozen, my nose was running, I felt frostbitten, and my feet were very sore and aching because of the enormous high heels that I had decided to wear that night. We warmed up with a glass of wine, and then another and another and another. I got so drunk that night, it was just dreadful. I was so sick; I threw up and passed out in his bed at his brother's house. Here was a guy I had only known for a few hours, and I was drunk and passed out in his bed. This could not possibly end well. I was in no condition to speak or even stand up.

I had a curfew that night of 11:30pm. I was not even awake at 11:30pm. My mom returned to her "detective" work, searching through my bedroom once again. She found Rob's number. She called and demanded to know where their house was. She had some friends of ours drive out and pick me up. I was humiliated. I remember her shaking her finger and angrily scolding me in front of Rob, his brother and sister-in-law, saying, "Shame on you, shame on you." I wanted to die; I was so embarrassed.

The drive home was pure hell. She yelled at me loudly, saying how irresponsible I was and that I was a very bad girl. Those statements were confirmation to me that I was a worthless curse and burden to my family. I felt like I was such a troublemaker.

I do take ownership that night. My behaviour was very irresponsible. I had a child at home and I disregarded my responsibility to him. I felt like my behaviour was not like what a mother should be. *I needed to be better*, I pondered, *but how? How could I be better?* I didn't know how. The guilt, shame and humiliation that followed and hung over me the next few weeks (not to mention the awful hangover that lasted three days) was dreadful. I thought for sure that Rob would never call me again. For all I knew, he was ridiculing me and thankful I was gone. I lashed out at myself. I again began to starve and mentally abuse myself.

To my surprise, he called again later that week.

Weeks turned into months, and Rob and I started seeing each other all the time, and really began to establish a relationship. I would take my son with me to visit him, and Rob would often come down to see us. We spent a lot of time together, and talked on the phone constantly. I gave my whole self to him. However, even during the first few months, sometimes things didn't seem quite right. He would make plans with me at certain times and then not show up. He would not be home at a time when he asked me to call. A part of me was suspicious, but I would tell myself that I found a guy who is accepting of me and my son, and that I should have nothing to complain about. I accepted any treatment he offered. I had such low self-esteem that I wondered, *Who else would ever want such a wretched girl like me and her child?*

In June of 1994, Rob told me that he needed to move out of his brother's place. He asked me to move in with him. I was happily surprised that he wanted to make a life with my son and me. I jumped at the idea.

I informed my mom I was moving out. Needless to say, the poop really hit the fan. We argued and fought constantly, and she and my sister actually threatened to not allow me to take my son with me. I raged, I screamed, I yelled, I lashed out and, as usual, I hurt myself. As my life became more difficult and unmanageable, the two of them "ganged up" on me, ridiculed me, and pointed out that my behaviour was exactly the reason why I shouldn't be allowed to take my child with me. I was scared. I wanted to run away, I wanted to kill myself. Despite their best efforts to prevent it, I eventually left with my son.

Rob found us an apartment not far from his brother's place in Ajax. He found some furniture at garage sales, and fixed the place up nicely for us. Moving in there, I felt so free. I was finally able to be a mom by myself, without my family's interference. I did things the way I liked. It was very liberating.

The summer came, and Rob worked with a new friend. However, most days he didn't come home. He would leave in the morning, and I wouldn't hear from him or see him until after midnight or the next day. The nights he did come home, he was very drunk. If I tried arguing with him, we would end-up in physical, violent fights. One thing I did not know about Rob when I moved in was that he had big problems with drinking and drugs. When I learned of his addictions, I felt like dying inside. I was frustrated, irritated and getting very angry. I demanded to know where he was and what he was doing. He never gave the answers I needed. There was little, and then no, communication between us. Frustrated, I often lashed out at my son. I yelled at him, and spanked him. Things got worse, and we had no money or food. We were both on social assistance. Rob took what little money we had and drank it away. What was I to do? In my scared and upset state, I figured that nobody else would ever want me, and that I had to put up with this lifestyle.

September came, and I went back to high school. Rob went back to school as well. Alex was on a waiting list for day care. When school started, I began leaving Alex with my mom for the week, and on weekends I took him back to our apartment. One Friday, before I left to pick him up, I told my mother that a spot became available at the daycare for my son starting on the following Monday. To my dismay, my sister and mother told me I couldn't have him! They said I was not fit to be a mother and that I could not take good care of him. I screamed on the phone that they couldn't have him. They both ridiculed me and told me I was an unfit mother. I went to pick him up, and he went into daycare that week.

I was not behaving as a fit mother. I did not know how. As I did the best I could, I was fighting against such horrors in my life and did not know how to handle them. I tried everything in my power. I did not feel I was worthy of having any other kind of life. I believed that this *was* life. This life resembled and mimicked the life I lived as a child. I knew how to "live" here and operate. I could function. I did not like it, but I believed this was life. This was my life.

I began Grade 11 again, and it started off well. Alex and I were on a schedule. We got ready for school and daycare, and our days had a routine. Consistency. However, the relationship with Rob continued to go downhill. I would find other girls' phone numbers in his pockets and wallet. Just like my mother, I became "Miss Detective" with these searching behaviours. When I confronted him with this evidence, we would get into big fights, and he would leave and not come home unless he was really drunk or had nowhere else to stay. I hated myself. I blamed myself. I wasn't pretty enough, not sexy enough. My food intake diminished more and more. I was less than 90 pounds, but I needed to take off more weight so he would love me. And so, the torture and abuse on myself continued. I felt that all our problems were my fault and that it was because of me that all of this was happening. It was quite the responsibility to take on, feeling as if I had created all the problems in my relationship and for being the reason that someone was not able to commit to me and be there for me. Heck, I was unable to commit to myself!

When Rob was sober, he was fun; he was kind and he was gentle. He would make promises to me that he would stop drinking and doing drugs. He promised to be a family man and be with us.

Sadly, I believed him.

October, 1994. I'm pregnant. Again.

Oh God, how could You? I asked. *How could You do this to me again? Have I not gone through enough? Why do you hate me God? Why?*

A part of me felt that it was OK, that it would change Rob. He would stay with me, help me and love me now. I waited for him to come home. I waited and waited. I finally called him and asked him to come home, saying I needed to speak to him. He flatly told me, "No." I could feel my heart racing. I told him that it was important. He refused to come home, and wanted to know over the phone. I told him I was pregnant. He asked, "Are you sure it's mine?" I felt the tears well up in my eyes. "Of course it's yours!" I yelled back. I hung up the phone, fell to the floor and cried. It wasn't supposed to go this way. This was not like a sappy movie scene at all. This was my life, and it was full of heartbreak, anguish and pain. Where was the love, the happiness, and the joy of being together?

Not much had changed after I told Rob that he was going to be a father. Telling him changed nothing, and our relationship did not change either. Rob continued his single way of life full of drinking, no responsibility and other women, while I continued in the insanity of my own life, thinking and praying -- "praying" in the form of scolding God for my life and focusing on my thoughts that Rob would change once the baby comes. I thought it would get better. Things continued to get worse.

Then I had a brilliant idea (or so I thought) -- I would leave him! I packed all my stuff, called Rob and told him I'm moving back home. He said "OK." I was hoping that he was going to say, "No, please don't go," but he didn't. In pain, I moved out. I didn't dare tell anyone I was pregnant again. Good grief, how could I? I did it again? I had gotten pregnant again with a different guy, and I was leaving him and moving back home. I wondered what kind of person I was.

I was away from Rob for about a week. I quit school again (it seemed that some sort of pattern was happening). Being home was worse, even more miserable than living with Rob. In desperation, I reached out and called him. No answer. The wheels in my head were spinning. I wondered what he was doing and who he was with. *Had he found someone else? What about me and the baby?* I felt that I needed to get back there to get a handle on things and try to control what he was doing. I moved back. He took me back. But unfortunately, nothing had changed.

My sister called me a few days after I had moved back with Rob. She asked me if I was pregnant, and I told her, "Yes." She said that she knew it, and that that was the reason I had gone back to him.

So there I was, back with Rob, and he was nowhere to be found. I grew accustomed to this inconsiderate treatment. I accepted this life. It was what I felt I deserved. Deep in my heart, I thought there might be some hope for the future; so, in my stubbornness, I held on and stayed.

In January of 1995, we were visiting my parents. Rob told them about my pregnancy. All during this time, I felt so dirty and degraded and disgusted with myself. The incredible shame that overcame me was unbearable; I could hardly look at my parents. All I kept saying to myself was, *How could I do this to them? Again?* I thought of all the heartache I had put them through throughout the years.

Rob and my dad spoke, and Rob agreed to marry me. I did not want to get married, but it felt like I had few options. Getting married seemed like a way to "save face" in front of my parents, and to save myself from further humiliation. We thought about eloping, but decided not to.

Rob and I went home that evening. He asked me, "Do you want to get married?"

I said, "If we do, I want to move back to Toronto." He agreed. On February 16, 1995, we were married. I thought of this as a new start. We were away from his old friends, he was married to me now, and a baby was on the way. I figured things were looking up.

Things didn't get better; in fact, they got worse.

I felt so alone. I felt a lot of responsibility with my son and the apartment and the pregnancy, and my new husband was never around. When he was home he was largely ignoring me, watching T.V. or napping.

To save money, we moved in with my parents. I was not happy about that, but this was familiar. Nothing much made me happy those days. There was no privacy in our house. I was becoming pleasantly plump as the pregnancy progressed.

I was grateful to God during both my pregnancies because at least I tried to physically take care of myself during those months. I ate well, took vitamins and went to the doctor regularly. Physically, I never felt better (except for the morning sickness).

My detective work continued with Rob. I constantly checked

his pockets for clues and anything else that I could find. I often found receipts to bars and phone numbers and even drugs. I destroyed everything I found. While I did this, I felt like I had Rob under control. He wasn't going to pull the wool over my eyes. I was determined to be one step ahead of him. I lived each moment on how I was going to catch him doing something bad. He wouldn't come to bed at the same time with me; I would lie awake wondering what he was doing. I would even sneak downstairs trying to catch him doing something bad. I didn't know what for, but I was on high alert for something.

There was more than enough evidence for me to acknowledge my fears of infidelity, but I was unable to face it. I turned a blind eye and told myself that there was always a reasonable explanation. Afterwards, he would treat me lovingly, which was something I craved and needed. I took as much love as I could get. It seemed like a good trade-off. I would find something bad and go through pain, and then get a few days of attention and love and acceptance. And so, life seemed to be going well for awhile.

On June 16, 1995, our baby girl was born. Corinne. Our beautiful, blonde, blue-eyed baby girl was a gift from God for both of us. I always prayed for a baby girl with blonde hair and blue eyes, and here she was. I vowed that my relationship with this baby was going to somehow be different. I was going to raise her my way.

Corinne was a sweet, quiet, loving child. She and I were very close. I couldn't believe the bond and love I felt for this little girl when she was born. She must have been just two months old when I started calling her Missy, and that loving name has stuck with her to this very day. Corinne has grown into a magnificent young lady. Through her journey, which has had challenges of its own, God has softened her beautiful heart to live a life towards Him. The openness we share is truly a gift from the Big Guy. The forgiveness and grace she is able to extend are gifts she has acquired with difficulty. When I see her strength and willingness to move forward in life with passion, and her ability in helping others, it blows me away and makes me proud to be her mother. I saw her helping at the homeless shelter, and once she even sacrificed her spring break to help children in another country. I feel such strong gratitude towards God for His love, and how He has worked behind the scenes of our lives.

Days and months went by with my new daughter and my three-year-old son, and we enjoyed our time together. We played and went to parks. We started to establish a routine and a strong family connection. My son loved his little sister, and she loved him too. They were like two little peas in a pod. I remember feeling that life was good and that my children loved each other. I wanted them to get along and respect each other. It was not going to be like it was with my own siblings. In my family of origin, sibling rivalry was out of control. It felt as though some members thought they were better than others, like we were trying to compete for a place. There was no respect in our relationships. I told myself, *No, my children are going to be different. We are all going to get along.* I vowed to be open and honest with my kids, and to talk to them about their feelings, problems, days, and what was going on in their lives. I also vowed to speak to them appropriately about sex and sexual abuse so that, if anything ever happened to them, they would not be ashamed to tell anyone.

I remember finally telling my mother about my childhood sexual abuse and the shame I felt. I was in grade four at the time, and I told my teacher what was happening to me. Finally, someone heard me. The Principal called in a social worker, my mother was called to come and talk to her, and I was called down from class. They questioned me about the abuse and all about the encounters. I thought, *Finally! Finally someone is going to help me and make it stop.* Unfortunately, my mother did not handle it well. She didn't tell my father. No charges were ever laid, and nothing happened. No one was confronted, and my cousins were never reprimanded for what they did to me. I felt crushed and defeated. I felt very guilty, like I had caused a whole bunch of trouble for no good reason. I went through all this pain, and nobody believed me. No one took care of me or seemed to care what happened to me. It was covered up, never to be spoken of again. The whole ordeal was swept under the rug. In my experience, when a child who has suffered sexual abuse finally gathers enough courage to tell someone, and the adults in their life do nothing to help them, the effects of the abuse are heightened and the child's soul is damaged even more. It causes devastating trauma to a young child. What I learned from this was that it didn't matter what others did to me -- I needed to "suck it up" and take it. I became ashamed of myself; I hated my mere existence. I carried the blame.

I have carried that shame and pain with me all my life. I learned that it was OK for men to take advantage of me. I learned that I had no right to refuse sexual violation. I had learned that you don't talk about sexual abuse, and that if you did, nothing happened to change anything. In situations like this, I learned that the injustice that happened to me was acceptable. Throughout my life, I carried on accepting the unacceptable.

Kids who have been abused will call out for help in other ways. Some will wet the bed, some will misbehave in school, some will become "bullies," some will be defiant, some will lash out and be destructive, some will run away from home, some will cry out by using alcohol, drugs or pornography, some will cut themselves, some will have poor grades in school from an inability to concentrate, some will seek out love from others by giving of themselves, some will become teen moms. And some will even become abusers themselves.

Friends, this topic needs to be spoken of freely, especially with our children. Teaching our kids about inappropriate touching, and to feel comfortable and safe enough in our families to discuss anything, is a first step in protecting them. It's our duty, as parents, to protect them by any means we can. This, in my opinion, is imperative.

Be open to see the "why" behind children's behaviour that we think is "bad," unacceptable or embarrassing. Look deeper. Ask questions without reacting. Be open yourself. Don't let shame stop you.

It has occurred to me that, through my life experiences, I had come up with coping skills in the form of compulsive and addictive behaviours in order to provide myself "relief" from traumatic events. Trauma in a child's life causes a breakdown in normal, healthy development and growth. I'm pretty sure some of you reading this can most likely relate to what I'm sharing.

I hear comments being made about people who suffer with addictions, and how they are stereotyped as "bad" people, losers, idiots, and people who take advantage of others; or they are said to "know better," but just choose to "act out" anyways. That last one has got to be my favorite. I'll be honest, I've used it with my husband in the past. Ouch.

Being a childhood sexual abuse survivor, and growing-up in a home with many different addictions, my behaviours become more and more clear to me. As I have changed in so many ways, there are still a few things that linger around when I'm not feeling safe. Take my rage, for instance. Oh boy, the incredible rage I have had in my life has been brutal. *Brutal!* Not to mention the trauma that my rage has caused in my own children's lives. Yuck! I realize it is an addictive behaviour I use to provide relief for myself when I feel I'm not being heard, or when I feel that I am losing control of my life. When I feel I'm in a situation that triggers uneasy feelings in me, my first response is to react, and I immediately want to scream, yell and throw something. When I am able to be present in the moment and focus on my emotions, I am better able to calmly speak to others and diffuse a potential traumatic disaster. Deciding to change my behaviour in that moment, and be aware of what is going on in me, is key to linking those reactions to the effects of the abuse.

I realized over the years that I also suffer from addiction due to the trauma the abuse caused in my life. I used to drink in the past. Not just a little glass of wine here or there; no, if I was to have a drink, it was going to be the whole bottle and more. I am thrilled to share that I have not had a drink of alcohol in over twelve years -- *Woot! Woot!* Today, I am better able to understand where this addiction was stemming from. It was stemming from the fact that I was traumatized and abused as a child, and that as that young child, I did not know how to provide help and safety for myself; in turn, as I grew up, I looked to things to relieve the pain inside me (as is often the case for those who have suffered abuse in their lives). We were emotionally, mentally and spiritually unhealthy people, making the best of what life had dealt us.

Trauma and addiction go hand in hand. Addiction is bondage. A bondage to self. It is not something we choose to do or want to do. However, whatever we may be addicted to -- be it drugs, alcohol, sex, porn, work, behaviours, busyness, cleaning or avoidance of life itself -- this coping actually carried us to where we are today, and in some way, has helped us to stay alive and cope with the horrors that we had encountered. I'm not saying these coping "skills" are OK; I'm saying that we, as a society, need to be more aware of what goes on in our families, our schools and churches. We have the power to break cycles in our own families by helping ourselves first. If there is a history of alcoholism, drug addiction or affairs in your family, you can bet your bottom dollar that the "isms" of addiction are lurking around. If there has been abuse not spoken about in your life or family, you can bet there's underlying issues affecting your life because of it. It's never too late to open that can of worms and let them out; you'd be surprised of the freedom that comes with it.

I could not understand why I was the way I was. Thankfully, today I have been made aware; and because I decided to stop running, stop hiding and turn around to face my demons, I am living a happy, healthier life. Life is not perfect, but I am able to live.

Please be aware that this abuse happens to so many people every day. In our own families, right under our own noses. The only way we can start to make a stop to this abuse is by talking about it.

I decided that this suffering was *never* going to happen to my children. I would be there for them, no matter what.

Because of the intense pain it caused me, I could have never imagined what benefits this sexual abuse would bring to my life. I could never have believed that God was, and had been, working behind the scenes in my favour all through this experience.

A couple of years went by, and our family of four hung on by the grace of God. The fighting, arguing, and my detective work continued. Unknowingly, I managed to create a threesome of me and my children against their dad. What I said went. The way I decided to raise the children went the way I wanted. Basically, Rob had no say in any decisions concerning this family. I honestly felt like a strong, capable woman who was holding this family together in our young lives. I was nineteen years old and I felt that I had enough experience in those nineteen years to take me a *long* way. I had this figured out. It was all under control. Rob's lifestyle of drinking, gambling, doing drugs, and seeing other women continued. I concentrated on the children, and turned a blind eye. I was in denial. Denial is often described as a shock absorber for the soul. When life is too difficult, and situations seem unbearable, an individual's way of responding to that life is with denial.

In December of 1996, at the ripe age of twenty-one, God saw fit for me to become pregnant again. *Well, Merry Christmas to me*, I thought. I was not happy about this new-found information. We were living at my parent's house, and there was already four of us. There was enough chaos just with us. The continued insanity of living with everyone else in the crowded house must have caused my parents untold disruption and frustration. They put up with my insanity, my craziness, my anger, and my lashing out at them (which was all stemming because I was angry at myself). They provided a roof over our heads, and gave much love and attention to my kids. I will say that I was, and still am, very grateful to God; very grateful that, despite the chaos of our lives, my children were given much love and attention from my parents. I did the best I could, but, because of my own problems and the bondage of myself, I could not always give my children everything they needed at the times they needed it. My parents were a huge help, and put up with all the confusion.

So, here I was, pregnant again. The overwhelming feeling of shame returned and came over me. I could not face the reality of knowing my parents would know what had happened again. What I had done! I wanted to run, scream and hide from my shame. Christmas day came, and Rob finally told my mom that I was pregnant again. I think he used the words, "bun in the oven." I wanted to vomit. Rob was happy about it. I was happy too, but I was also worried. This shame had always made me feel dirty and bad. I couldn't really tell if my mom was happy about it. I remember her coming over and hugging me, which made me feel even worse.

It didn't take long for the news to spread. Soon, the whole family knew. This was going to be another precious gift from God; however, I felt that it was a punishment by Him, and that He was disappointed in me. With this pregnancy, I grew round quickly. My skinny frame did not hide the fact that I was pregnant again. I took very good physical care of myself (I realize now that this was God's way of stepping in to save my life from the torture I was putting myself through).

Things started looking up when Rob got a job working down the street from our place. However, it was an afternoon and night shift, which was difficult for us. Money was coming in, and it was going out (most times before it even came in). Rob was often out, and his drinking continued. My loneliness continued. Life moved ahead on this roller coaster. I felt that that was how life is; that this was my life and I did not deserve anything better. I tried not to complain or say anything about how bad things were. After all, Rob accepted me -- what else could I dare ask for?

On August 14,1997, our second, beautiful baby girl entered this world. We welcomed Rebekah with love. Again, I felt the love wash over me. My sweet, sweet baby girl. Bekah is such a free-spirited young lady. She is so beautifully unique in her own special way. Even as a young girl she was very loving and affectionate. She displays such love and affection to our family and to our pets. Bekah is thoughtful, caring and selfless. She strives to look at the good in life (despite what is happening around her). Her heart has grown in Christ's love, and her determined dedication to follow Him shows in her acts of giving to others. She has even risen to the challenge of serving others in the United States during March Break. Bekah is a good "sounding board" for me when I'm getting flustered with my life, and she often repeats to me pieces of Scripture. She gives me back suggestions that I've given to her in the past. For a young teenage girl living through what this world has to offer, Bekah adds to my courage and strength to push forward in this life.

After Bekah was born, the family dynamic changed. Life was good and life was challenging, but we managed to carry on. My three wonderful kids grew together, establishing a relationship I was so blessed to witness. Here they were -- Alex, four; Corinne, two; and Rebekah, a few months old. I enjoyed them so much. We went out a lot, we played, and I really gave myself over to the joy of raising these children. Another blessing that had come about was that my dad agreed to let us fix up his basement for our own living space. It felt good to cook our own meals and have private family time. I could imagine it also felt good for my parents to have part of their home and privacy back.

Life remained the same for a while with the busy routine of raising small children. When Rebekah was two, we finally moved out of my parents' place and into a rented home down the street from them. What a great feeling it was to be independent. It felt like a new life. I felt that this was the answer to all our problems. Moving out, and having our own space, was freeing and wonderful. However, Rob's problems continued, and, to my sadness, we were fighting more over his drinking and lack of money. With our own house, Rob was able to have more friends over to drink. I will share that, over those next few months, I also joined in on the drinking. I would put the kids to bed, and drink with Rob. However, the family life the next morning was a punishment all its own. I needed to contend with three children and a hangover. I did this to be accepted by Rob, and so that I could have some time with him. It was also used as an escape from the pain I felt inside. Sadly, it was the price I was willing to pay to have some of his attention and some hours of "relief" from myself.

Thinking back, my desperation to be loved by someone, have attention paid to me and to feel acceptance, was a need. This need was so great that I would have gone to any lengths to have these things. I did what I needed to do to get them. My choices added to the guilt and shame I felt. I did not realize what my part was in all the problems. I often fantasized about other people's relationships. I compared Rob to other men I knew who I thought to be nice and wonderful and loving. I constantly put him down. Did I dare think that my behaviour was part of our crazy life? No way! After all, the focus was solely on what *he* was doing. His crazy life "out weighed" anything I was thinking or doing.

March, 1999

This was the biggest fight with Rob in all our lives together. He didn't come home one night. I did not hear from him, and I didn't know where he was. But deep down I knew. I was hurt, scared, angry, lonely and desperate. Needless to say, that was a sleepless night. When he came home the following day, I confronted him yet again. He again said that he was sorry and that it wouldn't happen again. I once again turned a blind eye to what he was doing. I could not face this latest rejection. I couldn't face the feeling of not being enough. My self-abuse started again, and it got much, much worse. I blamed myself for being too fat, for being too ugly, for not being adventurous enough. I was unable to make Rob happy. I mentally beat myself up. I told myself, *Look at what I did to this poor guy -- I destroyed his life*. I was nothing but a burden to him, as well as to everybody else. As I reminisce back to that year, it was one of the lowest points of my life. If it was not for my kids, I would have surely perished. I got more and more desperate, and wondered what I was going to do. I had reached the point of beyond despair.

The following week, Rob had planned a trip to go down east to visit his family, and I was very, very angry. I was left alone with my kids and my broken life; *I* had to try to gather the shattered pieces and put my life back together again. For Rob, getting up and leaving whenever he wanted was no problem. I was always there to take care of the kids and home. There was never any discussing with me when, and if, he could leave; he just did, and I allowed it. Mind you, there was never any discussing from me what happened concerning the kids, finances and what ever else went on, with him either. This was something we both not knowingly agreed on. At this point, I had reached an all-time low. I was so far in the ditch, with the muck over top me.

I had nowhere else to turn. I was defeated. I had nothing; nothing left to give. The one place I hadn't been turning my whole life came to mind. I had only one option: I needed to turn to God (even if it was in anger or desperation). I could no longer bear this life I was living. I was so alone, afraid and hurt. I had an enormous amount of guilt for blaming God for what had happened to me in this terrible life I was living (a life He supposedly gave to me). But how could I turn my face to Him? How was that possible? I carried such sin and shame. At this point, I didn't much care how it was going to be possible, I just knew that I needed to try something different -- all my previous efforts had failed. I fell to the floor, on my knees, and cried out to God. I turned my face from Him, and cried and cried. I called out to Him to help me, to please do something, because I couldn't anymore. I cried and called out to God to save me from this life that I was living. I told Him I wanted to die. I told Him I was angry at Him for doing this to me. I also told Him how sorry I was. With this, I finally surrendered. I surrendered myself, and came to terms with how I could no longer live this way and how I was unable to do anything to change Rob or my life. I came to the conclusion that I did not have the power to make someone else do something, or be what I wanted him/her to be. I called out to God. My cry was desperate. It was angry. It was empty. I said, "God help me, I can't do this anymore. Please do something. Stop this life, stop this life." I got to a point where the tears stopped. I felt like the world stopped; the rage and thrashing of my soul ceased. There was quietness, there was peace...

I love thinking back over the years on how my relationship with Christ has evolved. It makes me smile, and I feel amazement to the incredible trust I feel being left in His care. As I journey back, I'm blown away by the miracles that occurred right under my nose; how God was there the whole time. During the times of desperation and grief, He carried me. I made it here today because of Him, and Him alone.

I am nothing without Him. I was a lost soul running wild. God worked behind the scenes. He walked along side me, even though I never did seek Him. He was there. No matter how I cursed Him, ridiculed or blamed Him for my life, He never, *ever* left me. As I write this, tears come to my eyes. I have this feeling in my chest; it makes me catch my breath in awe. He has never left me. Never abandoned me. How do I know this? I know because of some sketchy situations I put myself in, and how I came out of those situations safely. My family has always been kept safe, held together, protected. And for the fact that I am here today, alive and well -- that, my friends, was no one other than God.

What kind of a God is this? There is no other, no other god, who loves as He loves. No other god sticks around while he is being abused and blasphemed. No other god has made such a sacrifice as He did for me. No other. No other has picked me up, placed my feet on solid ground and held me. He always held me. Through my abuse, it was He who held me. Through my self-hatred, He loved me. Through my heartache in life, He, and He alone, provided the comfort for me. No matter how many times I screwed up, did He ever leave me? Abandon me? Forsake me? Never.

What He did was *miraculous*! He dusted me off, polished me and loved me, no matter what I did, or didn't, do. And I'm so excited for what He's continuing to do in my life today.

This opportunity to proclaim His incredible, undeniable love for me, for *us*, is just one example.

No matter what, God stays with us. He never said it was going to be easy, but He did promise we would never be alone. And although we may feel He's nowhere to be found at times, He is working out all of our situations -- our hurts and our pains -- for our benefit. I like to describe it as a gift. When I go through tough, challenging times, I *know* that God is going to have such a gift for me at the end of it; a gift of growth and of more connection with Him; a gift of a cleaner, more *loving* heart.

He stays with us by providing the stepping stones through our challenges. He stays with us by giving us enough courage and strength to keep moving forward, even though we may not know at the time that it's Him who's giving this to us. Sometimes He uses friends, family or even complete strangers; and, in my case, my story.

Friends, without my past, I would have never turned to Him. I would never have the blessings of an amazing husband and awesome, spectacular kids. I would not love myself today. I would not be able to share my life openly and honestly with you. I would not be able to say with confidence that, no matter what, God is always with us and is even closer to us in our darkest days.

When we decide to turn our lives over to God, there are some actions and thinking that need to change. Things cannot be done only from the outside. Changing needs to take place on the inside of us. We need to know how we behave and treat others. How do we operate? What are our true beliefs? What is our thinking like? We must take all of these things into consideration when we are choosing to change our life and make our living and contribution to our families and society a good one. We can have Bibles, memorized Scripture, self-help books, and all kinds of therapy; but, if we don't change what needs changing (and that is ourselves), then all these things are useless. All of these things simply act as tools. God is our true guide; He shows us, but He doesn't do the work for us. We need to get our butts in gear and go for it. *We need to do it!* No, it's not easy, and yes, it's scary, but what do we have to lose? If we are not happy already, what is there to lose by changing? If we've picked up self-help books or CD's, then we are searching for a change. There's a disturbance to the life we are living; there is a disturbance within us, and that is not OK. We want more; we want better. Friends, this is a great start, but it doesn't stop by just reading and telling others in our lives to read and change. *We* need to *be* that change. We need to start to change regardless of what others in our lives are doing or not doing. We have one life to live. One. God gave this life to us, and the struggles that happen along the way become our platforms to walk across and grow. Don't just get those good books and place them on the shelves -- read them, *do* what they say, and become who God created you to be. There are no problems or situations that God cannot deliver you from. Most of the time, it is ourselves that hold us back from that deliverance. We don't go the extra mile; we quit when it becomes tough, sabotaging our own breakthrough.

The first step in my journey started with a book my dad had lying around at home for years. Now, I'd like to share some very important memories I have of my dad. My dad is in his seventies now -- a strong, hard working man. When I was younger (around six or seven, maybe older) my dad used to take me to church. No one else in my family wanted to go; not my mom, nor my siblings. My mother would force me to go to church with my dad so that he wouldn't get upset. I used to resent this terribly. So, every Sunday morning, off I went with my dad to church.

Thinking back, my dad used to try to hold the family together. He tried to bring God into the family, but there wasn't enough "reinforcement," and he gradually gave up. I see my dad so differently today. I see him in a whole different light: in God's light. He was doing the best he could with what he had. Dad tried to fix our family's problems with self-help books and therapy, but to no avail. Our family problems remained and grew worse.

As my dad and I visited many different churches and

experienced many different denominations over the years, I remember going to Sunday school and having a workbook that my dad bought me from church. I sill have that workbook. I wrote in it when I was young. I felt a connection to God when I wrote in that book, even at that young age. Sadly, over time, and as life got more difficult, the connection got clouded and weaker. To this day, I thank God that Dad kept that door of faith open for me (even if it didn't stay open for long). Dad taking me to church, even against my will, laid a foundation and planted seeds that would be harvested in due time. I believe God knew this.

It would be years later, upon moving out, when I found that workbook and a few other of Dad's books. Later, on that day of despair (when Rob had decided to take a trip to visit his family), I finally reached for one book in particular. I couldn't get enough of what I read. As I read and read, I felt lighter and lighter. I started to see God through a different lens. I knew there was much changing that needed to take place, and I truly believe that God gave me the wisdom to know that it wouldn't happen overnight.

I continued on, and, from that day forward, I began to feel differently. My focus came off of what was happening in my life and in my marriage to Rob, and went largely to Jesus. The week that Rob was away turned out to be a great benefit. God used this time to really stir up the "dust" inside me. I also recall the peace I felt that week. I was patient with the kids; I took time to be with them and be present with them in the moment.

What started to happen during that week was something I cannot fully explain. I know, in that time, I made a decision to follow God. For me, that was *huge*! I agreed to follow God, the same God I loathed and blamed for all my problems. He was the same God who seemed to be punishing me all the years of my life. This was the same God to whom I made a decision to turn my life over. I wondered if I was crazy. *Maybe*, I remember thinking. But what did I have to lose? At this point in my life, nothing. I had nothing to lose.

I was new at this following Jesus stuff, and I knew that I had made a decision to change my old ways and behaviour, and that I should buckle up and hang on (for it was not going to be an easy ride). So, the journey started, and the peace I immediately felt was so refreshing. I wondered why I had waited so long to do this.

The days turned to weeks, and weeks to months, and I put my time in with God. I started reading. Daily, I read His word in the form of the Bible, along with a daily devotional from the same author of the first book that had helped set me up to meet Jesus. I got into the habit of reading, journaling, praying and speaking to Him throughout the day. I began to feel as if He was truly my only friend. He was the only One I could be totally honest with about my feelings and what was really happening in my life. This new-found way of living did not exempt me from the horrors of what my life was like. However, I didn't feel so alone this time. I felt like I finally had a friend who understood me. A friend that I could go to at any time of the day. A friend who would listen to my rants and complaints without judgement.

As I continued on my journey, I felt free. It was as if, somehow, all our issues were gone. I was feeling alive and on top of the world. I suspect I had some skewed thinking that nothing could harm me. It's as if I thought: *If everyone would just read their Bibles, get up early to pray and devote time to God, then everything in our lives would be just perfect.* As I carried on this way for some time, I did not realize that I was creating in my family the illusion that our lives were perfect. I was in such denial of my reality. I longed for life to be perfect, and I created in my head, and for others who saw us from the outside, this illusion of perfection. I realized that I had done exactly as my parents had done. I realized I was hiding our problems from the outside world. Nobody spoke about what was really going on behind closed doors.

I now realize that I lied, and created something that was not real. I projected to my children that we need to be, and are, the perfect Christian family. We were following Christ now, and we shouldn't have any problems anymore. *No, no, no we do not,* we told ourselves. If any of my children had a problem or issue, we would just suck it up, tough it out and put on a happy face. *Or better yet,* I thought, *deal with problems my way, and everything will work out great. Trust me, I know better,* I thought. I was the one reading the Bible every day; I was the one getting to know God.

I took our children and myself to church every Sunday, with or without their father. I knew the better way. I now also realize that, back then, I got on my "high horse," and I didn't know why. God knew why, but I was sitting there dictating and manoeuvring my little children's feelings around to suit my needs, and to ensure it all looked perfect to the outside world. I should also mention how I was behaving towards Rob. I was either giving him the "silent treatment," blaming him for negative things that happened, or making sure I told him what he was doing wrong (coupled with my knowledge of how it should be done properly). Whatever the situation was, I was quick to put my "two cents in." I was a new person now, full of anger of a different kind; anger that motivated me to have a heart as hard as stone, and to not allow anyone to hurt me or walk all over me ever again. With this anger, rage grew stronger day by day. In this state, I started to deal with the hurts and wrongs being done to me with violent acts of rage. I threw anything I could get my hands on -- stuff went flying through the house or out the door. The screaming at the top of my lungs at Rob, or the kids, was disgraceful. Rob often walked out of the house when the fights or arguments got this out of control. In fact, walking out while there was any family issue or situation between us happened many, many times. It was a set pattern, it seemed to me. This used to push me over the edge; I was so out of control that I did not know what to do.

I cannot begin to imagine how afraid my children must have felt. I wondered how my behaviour had gotten worse since God appeared on the scene.

It got to a point where I could pull myself together fairly quickly after an outburst. I would apologize to my kids for what I had just done or how I had behaved, the little ones would say, "It's OK," and we would carry on. And so, this life of insanity, for all of us, continued for years and years.

And so, years went by, and we were surviving. It often felt like we merely existed in thin air. Then, Rob went through a very challenging time early in the year 2001. He lost his brother. With this death and loss, something changed in Rob. In the month of October 2001, Rob quit drinking and drugs. *Yes, he quit!*

At first, I could not believe what was happening. Rob shared with me how he did not want to drink anymore, and how he wanted to be a better father and husband. These were words I had longed to hear all my life. The love that I had longed to feel all my life was suddenly happening. Was this a dream? The happiness I felt was unreal. *Well, thank God,* I thought, *Rob is finally changing his ways.* I thought my problems were all over with this development. And for a little while, they really were over (to some degree). Financial issues continued; I could not understand why we continued having these financial pressures when the money spent on drinking had come to an end. This frustrated me. But this was something else, and just how life was, I told myself.

During the next few months and years, Rob and I seemed to be establishing closeness, and, at times, even had fun together. He was more involved with the kids, and spent more "fun time" with them. He became Mr. Wonderful. He brought me gifts, and seemed to be more present in the relationship. He played with the kids, and was more available for us.

In my happiness, I delved deeper in my relationship with God. I thanked Him endlessly for how my life had been improving. However, during these times, I continued on abusing myself. I limited my food intake and I exercised to the point of sheer exhaustion. I continued on with my suspicions of my husband; I continued to not trust him, and refused to "get too close" with him.

My trust in God grew, and I came to believe that God was taking care of us. I started to devote more of my life to Him. I woke up early every morning to spend time with God and pray. It was time I looked forward to; my "alone" time. I spent time in prayer with God. Prayer, to me, began to seem so different from my past. My prayers were not rehearsed, or ones I had learned at church or from books. These prayers were from my heart. They were moments of talking to, and with, God. And to my amazement, I became more open and honest about my concerns and my lack of understanding in areas of my life that just didn't seem to be working. As I continued to nurture this relationship, I felt God asking me to start analyzing areas of my life that needed attention.

This had nothing to do with others. I no longer felt as if my life was a mess because of everyone else. This affliction had everything to do with me. I evaluated how I chose to speak to others on a daily basis. I tried to reduce the profanity that had previously escaped my lips without my control. I thought about, and changed, what I chose to watch on TV and the genre of music I chose to listen. I started to replace the things in my life that blocked my way to Jesus with things that brought Him glory and enhanced my relationship with Him. Something inside me started to long for closeness with God and doing what was right for Him.

As I was starting to get to know God more intimately, I was

also getting to know this other side of Rob, and I started to really like it. However, we seemed to be stuck on the roller coaster. When times were good, they were really good. I was so "in love" with Rob, and so "in love" with the appearance of being a perfect family. After good times, our world would come crashing down, and I could not understand why this kept happening.

If there seemed to be an issue with paying bills, or I asked about money that was being spent, the fighting would start anew. Rob would pull away and ignore me. The loneliness I felt, even though Rob was right there in front of me, gave me such heartache. When that hurt and pain started, the "crazy lady" who was locked inside me would come out. I would push Rob away, "close up," and isolate from him and the world. I "acted out" in frustration by throwing things, swearing, and endlessly threatening to end the marriage. Up and down, up and down, our family went. Year after year, things remained in the same pattern. For some reason, we all held on tightly through each catastrophe. I took the good with the bad. *After all*, I thought, *this is life. My life.*

Throughout these years, and through my loneliness, I escaped with emotional affairs. I was unfaithful to Rob in many ways. I longed to be loved and cared for. I talked to and relished in the attention I received from others, men in particular. What I wanted, craved and longed for from Rob, I subconsciously went out searching for. I continued to fantasize about Rob finally giving me what I needed and wanted: the love and attention I so desperately craved. Conversations and "get-together's" I would have with others, I fantasized to be with Rob. This need for love grew inside me. I wanted so much for someone to love and care for me. Sadly, I did not understand the love I wanted. Because of my distorted thinking, and due to the childhood sexual abuse, I came to believe that sex was love. Sex was attention, acceptance and love. This is not so. Not so at all. It has taken me years to understand what love is and to change my faulty thinking about it. So, with my own unfaithfulness to Rob in the form of tea times and conversations with people of the opposite sex, I continued to give myself attention and "love" in order to "hold on" another day. I did not see anything wrong with the nonsense I was doing. After all, I was feeling fulfilled (which, in turn, made me feel more at ease with my husband). I was receiving what I wanted, and that was attention. This attention made me feel worthy, and no matter how God nudged me and clearly pointed out in His word and in my heart that this was not OK, I pleaded with God and "prettied it up" to make it OK. It was never OK. I didn't understand that the love I craved was not from another human being, but from God. I needed to know the unconditional love of God in order to love myself. Even after deciding to give my life to Christ, there were those old behaviours I was not able to see in myself due to the fact that I was still using them to feel whole; to fill that emptiness, that longing, inside me that needed filling up. I believed that searching outwards to others would eventually fulfil that need. This is "worldly love." This is empty "love," temporary "love." Just as those who suffer addiction use substances, this was a substance I craved, and this "love" and attention from others would give me a temporary "fix" to continue on my day. I became addicted to the feeling of needing that "love." Over the years, I was rudely awakened by God to learn that this is not love. Love is as it is described in God's word:

> *Love is patient and kind. Love is not jealous, it does not brag, and it is not proud. Love is not rude, is not selfish, and does not get upset with others. Love does not count up wrongs that have been done. Love is not happy with evil but is happy with the truth. Love patiently accepts all things. It always trusts, always hopes, and always remains strong. Love never ends...* (1 Cor. 13:4-8).

Learning to love this way requires a lot of getting to know yourself, and requires that you allow God to come in and clean you up from the inside out. I heard it explained to me this way from a friend: think of our insides covered with blackness. The blackness is all our sin, our wrong choices, our worldly living. As we commit ourselves to God and allow Him to come into our hearts and clean up all that gunk, He then creates light inside us. The more we turn from our sinful ways and worldly living, the more we are filled with God's light. This light then produces the true love we all crave to have. In turn, we are then able to give that love to others.

As the days went by, and guilt tried to surface over me, I continually reminded myself that I was lucky that Rob took me in, so I must be grateful for that fact and endure whatever came my way. These crazy times seemed like my punishment for my wrongdoings in life. With that, I took each day as it came and decided to make the most of it. Life continued on and seemed to be manageable. It *felt* manageable. After all, I was keeping up with housework, caring for our children, working, and I was also the Chair of the Parents' Council at the children's school. All of this kept me busy and away from dealing with the truth and reality of what was really going on in this crazy life. I accepted whatever attention Rob was willing to give to me, our marriage, and our family.

I started to feel restless. I was feeling that something was missing, that something was not right. *Aha!* It came to me. We needed to buy our own house! This was what the problem was: renting the apartment we stayed in seemed "not good enough." We, or rather, *I*, needed more stability -- a sure thing, like a house of our very own. *Yes*, I convinced myself, *this is the answer to all our problems.* The kids needed their own bedrooms, their own backyard, their own house. And so, we went to work on this. This distraction made me feel good. I was happy. We would be as good as the neighbours and the rest of the world once when we bought our own house. I decided that this was what we needed in order to feel good. This was going to solve *all* of our problems.

In November of 2006, we bought our house (which did not come easy at all). It created more financial stress than we could have ever imagined. But, like with everything else, we rolled with it. After a few months in our new home, we all felt ecstatic with our own place. The kids had their own rooms, and, for the time being, this masked our pain and hurt. It covered up whatever was going on right underneath our noses. It seemed as though we were happy.

The seasons passed, and we had company over all the time (in the form of neighbours and friends). Our home became the "hangout" for kids and parents alike. This kept me busy and out of reality. I cooked, cleaned, catered and provided a place for others to come and stay. From the outside, things, once again, looked perfect. We were complimented many times on how great our family was, how wonderful our children were, and how funny and witty Rob was. Everyone got such entertainment from him. He was the life of the party with his quick, and sometimes sarcastic, jokes. He made us laugh. I thought that life could not get better than this.

I saw that our kids were excelling in school and with their peers. We went to church, our girls became alter servers, and our son played guitar in the choir. Rob came to church with us every week. Life seemed perfect. But I wondered, *Why do I feel this nattering, underlying pain in my gut that something just isn't right?*

Rob is home from work today, and as I sit here typing away, I glance over at him, feeling compassion, disbelief, relief and true love. Not that gooey romantic love you read in books or see on TV, but that real love that feels like you would choose it over again. Writing this has caused memories to come flooding back from where we started, up to where we are today. Honestly speaking, so much has changed; and then there are those things that haven't changed and probably never will change. It's been a long haul, but, day by day, we continue to muddle through.

But, back then, I felt that things weren't right. Underneath this perfect-looking family and busy schedule, I felt an ugly evil lurking. It felt like the evil would rear its ugly head every now and again, but I would ignore it, accept it, and basically club it over the head (like in the game Whack-A-Mole). It would hide in its hole again. We would fight, I would threaten divorce, and after a few days and apologies, we were back on the track to Happy-Ville. And life would feel good and normal again. The pattern repeated itself.

The evil that I speak about is, in my opinion, something that plagues our entire nation and the whole world. It stays hidden (to some degree), but at other times and places, it is very open and accepted.

Over the years of our marriage, I would notice behaviour from my husband that society deems "OK." It didn't feel OK for me. I would see him look at other women. It killed me inside. When I confronted him about this each time it happened, he would deny it and we would fight until I came around and apologized for accusing him. I knew in my heart that what I saw and felt was true, but I could not understand how to make him confess to me. I wanted very much to make him stop. I wondered how to do it.

The use of pornography in our home during the early years of our marriage didn't seem right to me. I felt a lot of guilt. I felt ashamed that my husband was not satisfied with me. I thought he needed these movies to be with me because I was not good enough. Hence, the battle with trying to change my appearance continued and progressed. Our marriage started to decline rapidly and differently this time. We came to a point in our church life and in our marriage that it was time to seek outside help. I believe it came to this point because a part of me could not, and would not, bear this any longer. I had caught him too many times, and made it known that I knew something was wrong. With this realization, my health started to go downhill again and I became less present with my family. I became consumed and obsessed by what was happening. I could not think of anything else except the betrayal I felt and the unworthiness of not being good enough for my husband. I felt that I had let him down. The crazy started again with my eating difficulties and excessive exercising.

We started seeing our priest (who was also a marriage counsellor). I felt that we finally had some help. We went to see him weekly, and, with each session, I would leave feeling irritated and that my concerns were not being heard. I felt like *I* was the one causing trouble in our marriage. I shared with our priest how hurt I was that my husband looked at other women. When I say "looked at other women," I do not mean a short glance; no, I mean a good, long look up and down, and at specific parts of the body. The priest would reply that it was normal to glance at other people and accept their beauty. *Ha*, I thought. This was more than glancing and accepting beauty, this went far beyond that. When I pleaded my case for either one of them to help me and stop this from happening, I felt like I was dying inside. Our priest often comforted Rob and would make excuses for his behaviour, and tell me how wonderful Rob was. The frustration grew. The resentment felt like poison in my blood, killing me slowly, minute by minute. *What am I going to do*, I wondered. Who was going to help me? Months went by like this, filled with heartache, confusion and bitterness.

One evening, Rob came home with flowers and a note saying how sorry he was for everything. He quoted me some scripture from the Bible that said,

> *If another follower sins, warn him, and if he is sorry and stops sinning, forgive him. If he sins against you seven times in one day and says that he is sorry each time, forgive him* (Luke 17:3-4).

He asked me out to dinner so that we could talk, and I agreed to go. I was longing for some comfort and "normal" life. We went out that night, Rob said all the right things, and I was grateful to God that my husband finally came around to see this situation from my side. He assured me that he wanted this marriage and that he loved me and wanted to work on us. I forgave him, and decided to recommit myself to him. We committed and continued going to marriage counselling. It seemed as if we had beaten whatever was trying to bring us down. I felt like I won him back. He was finally mine.

Months went by, and we were getting along beautifully. I felt I could not be any happier than I was during those months. Rob continued to work late hours and nap constantly, but he also gave himself to me and the kids. He *seemed* to be more present than ever.

However, during those months, there was a constant gnawing in the pit of my stomach. I couldn't quite put my finger on it. One beautiful, sunny, warm Saturday in May of 2010, I awoke extra early and spent time with God. I quieted myself, prayed and read God's Word. I felt this heat arise in me, and I immediately got down on my knees and raised my hands and prayed. I said out loud, "God, something is not right. I feel something is very wrong here. I am making a decision to surrender Rob and my marriage into Your hands. I have no control, and I cannot do this anymore." With that prayer, I felt like the weight of the world was lifted from my shoulders.

That day, the children, Rob and I were committed to helping a friend move. Rob planned to be home to lend his pick up truck to carry furniture. He came home, all was well, and he went to shower.

For a few weeks leading up to this day, I had noticed Rob continually using a phone we had (one with Internet access). I felt suspicious, but, once again, turned a blind eye and disregarded that gnawing feeling in the pit of my stomach. I thought that that was weird, but trusted him anyway. After all, the incredible changes in him over the past few months were heavenly. This day he was in the shower for quite some time. I had gone ahead to our friend's place which was not far from our own place. I was over there for a couple hours, and started to wonder where on earth Rob was. I decided to come home to check to see where he was. As I came in, he was heading out to meet me. I decided I was going to run up and use our washroom before heading over there again. So up I went for a pee. As I sat there, I looked into a book bin we had. In there, was the phone. With shaking hands, I picked it up and turned it on. I didn't know exactly what I was looking for, but I knew in the back of my mind that Internet was accessible from this device. At first I thought, *No Chris, don't go there.* But I did. This was very old and, to me, bad behaviour on my part. I did not want to go back to any old ways. However, I opened up the web page and went to the history. To my utter disgust and dismay, numerous porn sites came up. My heart was racing so fast that I almost threw-up. I was in disbelief; I did not know what to do. Something inside me said, *It is finished now.* I didn't know what that meant or where it was coming from. I was in despair, with no one to whom I could turn. At that moment, I heard my eldest daughter come up the stairs. I opened the bathroom door, and asked her, "Corinne, when you open the history on this web page, does it show you the right web sites that were recently used?" She said, "Yes." I almost passed out. I then said to her, "I need help. I need to know if this is right. Please check this for me." So, unfortunately, I sucked that poor child into the vortex that was spinning all around us. She took the phone and said, "Yes mom, someone was on these sites. Who had it last?" I knew exactly who just had it last: her father, my husband. The anger bubbled up from the depths of my insides; I was shaking uncontrollably, and it was like all of our years of craziness came flooding in. All the signs of infidelity, all the unexplainable events and mood swings -- this explained it all. The other women, the looks, the betrayal. My world was splitting into a million pieces, and there was nothing I could do about it.

Sadly, Corinne encountered that trauma and experienced the hurt along with me. I saw the anger well up in her eyes. I could feel her little heart turn to stone. I couldn't help her; I had just exposed her to this ugliness, and I couldn't even help myself. We sat together in my bedroom, stunned at this realization.

Rob was downstairs during all of this. He came up and asked us, "What's up? Everything OK?" With a shaky voice I said, "Yup." He stood there looking at me, and I at him. He went back downstairs. A few minutes later, I descended and walked past him as he reached out to grab my hand. I quickly pulled away, and told him through clenched teeth, "Don't you ever touch me again." We stared at each other for a few seconds before he stood up, went to the washroom, and closed the door. I stood there frozen. He got out a few minutes later, came down the stairs, and, without looking at me or saying a word, walked out of the house. He was gone for hours. I had gone to bed long before he got home.

I didn't know what to think, how to feel, or what I was going to do. I told no one of this horror I found. Something was going on inside me during these two days. I cried out to

God with all my heart. I cried and cried until I had no tears left. I couldn't eat, sleep or think straight. The kids knew something was seriously wrong. Corinne carried this heavy burden inside herself, and the other two knew there was trouble brewing. The next day, I sat my other two children down and shared with them what I had found. Corinne decided to tell them exactly how it all "went down." We all experienced anger, rage, disbelief, and utter shock. I had decided that this was the last straw. I thought I was going to divorce him. I had finally had enough.

God, where are You?

I sat and reminisced of the years past. All the signs were there that there was always a problem. There was a big lack of intimacy between the two of us. We did not have the ability to communicate effectively, and we had a lack of passion for our marriage. I remembered the power struggles and lack of commitment, not to mention the continuous flirting and gawking at other women. I felt particularly hurt by his rejection of spending alone time with me. *I saw all of this*! Why was I so blind? I felt so stupid, like a fool. A blind fool.

I spent the next couple of days hurting, crying in anger and feeling sorry for myself. I knew I was only going to get through this with God's help. I slowly crawled back to living. I gathered what little strength and feelings I had left, and reached for my Bible. I cried, I prayed and I asked God to help me. I didn't know what else to do. I wanted to die. The pain and hurt inside me was so heavy and so great that I couldn't bear it any longer. As I opened my Bible, it fell to John 16:33 (New King James Version):

These things I have spoken to you, that in Me you may have peace. In the world, you will have tribulation; but be of good cheer, I have overcome the world.

What? I said to myself. *Peace? Be of good cheer?* Did God know and see what was happening in my life at this time? Our family, my life, my *world*, had fallen apart. *How* could I ever be of good cheer? This was the ultimate heartache. Total rejection. But still, something inside me clung to God. There was no other power out there that could help me or my family now. No matter what *I* did, it was no use; a series of efforts gone in vain.

My first contact with Rob after the discovery was interesting. He had come home Sunday morning. The kids and I had just come home from church. In all my pain, I had dragged myself and the kids out of the house and to church. It was the right place for me to be at the time.

As we came home, he was sitting on the front porch. I looked at him, and a feeling came over me; a feeling with the knowledge and freedom to accept that this had nothing to do with me. I walked up and sat in front of him. I said to him, "For the first time in my life, I feel free. You're a sick man and you have a problem. I don't know what it is, but you need help." He replied, "I don't know what's wrong with me." My heart was crushed. I said back to him, "I can't help you." I went inside, and that was the last of our conversation. He got in his truck and vanished until Monday morning.

In the midst of this, I was still helping my friend pack up her house and move. I'm grateful for the distraction I had. She had asked me if everything was Ok; I was honest and said, "No." Her and her husband noticed that I had removed my wedding ring.

My wedding ring was very sacred to me. It was a vow I didn't want to take at the time, but I *did* take it, and I am a firm believer in no divorce. I firmly believe that there is nothing, no problems, that cannot be helped and tackled with God's help. I also believe that both partners must be willing to seek God for guidance and direction.

They, too, realized something was seriously wrong. They did not pry, but told me that if there was anything I needed, they were there for me, the kids and Rob too.

Rob came home the next morning, and asked if he could speak to me. He asked me to please help him find some phone numbers for a place he could get help. I reluctantly helped him. Once again, I dragged Corinne into all this mess and asked her to help me find these numbers. She and I printed out some telephone numbers for him and left him to it. It was a holiday Monday, so no one was available for Rob to speak with.

Thinking back to that day, I felt compassion for this man. I was angry at myself for feeling that way, so I covered it with anger. But there he was, like a lost little boy who was being punished for being bad. The kids did not speak to him -- they followed my lead on this situation. My lead was: "no speaking to the 'bad' man." I treated Rob harshly. I moved out of our bedroom and into a spare room we had in the house. I was repulsed and could not sleep in that bed of ours.

I had no contact with him over the next three weeks. Over that time, I would hear Rob come from work, shower, and leave the house. However, we did have some small talk as to what he was up to. By God's grace, he found a fellowship that dealt with the nature of the problem he was going through. I did not believe in such nonsense. My thinking was stuck in the "you should know better" and "you choose to be this way and do the repulsive acts you do" mode. I started to think, *Here I am with all the broken pieces of my heart and dealing with the family, while you are out there making friends and getting help that you think you need for misbehaving?* Oh boy, the volcano was going to erupt and it wasn't going to be good for anyone.

The next few days were spent finding and burning any evidence of our marriage. Pictures, letters and cards from the years passed, I burned in our fireplace. I wanted to rid myself of him and any piece of history I shared with him throughout this fraudulent life. It was as if this nightmare would go away as long as I could remove any trace of this marriage. Needless to say, it did not; in fact, our lives, mine in particular, spiralled totally out of control. The emotions that bubbled up from my insides were so overwhelming that I thought I was going to die. I felt lost, abandoned and humiliated. By this time, I was not looking after the kids or the house. I slept all day and, in my waking hours, isolated from family and whatever friends I had at the time. I became so self-absorbed in my shame and feelings that I had no time or energy to care what happened next.

I awoke one morning -- it was June 2010 -- and I prayed, and I journaled. I asked God -- actually, I *told* God -- of my decision. I had decided that I was going to divorce Rob. This was something I would just not tolerate. I was not willing to tolerate this nonsense of sharing my husband with other women. In the flesh or in the mind. So, this beautiful, sunny day in June, I awoke and journaled and justified my plea to God. After all, His Word clearly states we may divorce for sexual immortality. *Whoo!* I was off the hook. This was my "green light" to get rid of this man, and this burden, from my life. I would be free! Rob, as far as I knew and convinced myself, was the ruin of my life. He created all this craziness. The abuse, the instability -- this was Rob's doing. And now, I had the "OK" to end it all. Well, praise God for this way out!

As I journaled, I was relieved that this was going to be the day of freedom.

Rob came to my room that very morning. He asked to speak to me. I thought to myself, *God, you are working this out in my favor.* The kids were at their friend's house; we had the house to ourselves. I was actually happy to speak to Rob this particular morning, for I was going to cast him out of this house and family. Before we spoke, Rob handed me a book; he went on to explain what the book was, and how he felt compelled to buy me one and give it to me to read. He said he actually had it for a few days before he had the nerve to give it to me. I accepted it. I still hadn't said a word. Rob asked if he could go out and get us a coffee before we talk. I shrugged my shoulders, and off he went. When he came back, we sat out on the back deck, and, for the first time in all fifteen years of marriage, *he* spoke. I said not one word. Rob went on to apologize for his actions; he was very honest and told me exactly what he was up to during the years of our marriage and before our marriage. The unexplained missing money now had a place. The unexplained feelings that something was wrong were justified. The loneliness and emptiness in our marriage was explained. I sat there mortified and sick to my stomach. I could not say a word. The infidelity was heart wrenching. I was stunned. All I could do was ask God to reach down and touch my heart because I thought I was going to die. As I closed my eyes and prayed, I felt a peace and serenity come over me -- a wave of heat passed from the top of my head and through my body; and what it left behind was a heart of compassion. As Rob spoke, I saw him not as my husband, but as a poor little boy who was tormented and plagued by the fierce abuse of abandonment, physical trauma and emotional trauma growing up. I sat there and listened to his life and, for the first time in my life, I felt true compassion for another human being.

Compassion was not a feeling I had acquired in my life. I was cold and bitter towards others who had problems or issues with addictions or in their marriages. I was quick to offer advice and tell them how to handle it. I saw these people as idiotic human beings who could not pull their lives together. I had no time or patience for these "type" of people. None, whatsoever. Disgusted and angry at myself for feeling compassion to this man sitting before me, I clung to God for strength.

As Rob continued to share his life with me, my agenda, and what I had to say, took the "back burner" for the time being. We spoke, *he* spoke, for over five hours straight. We have never communicated in this manner. We barely ever spoke for five minutes at a time, let alone five consecutive hours of Rob speaking! Towards the end of this talk, I did share with Rob what my decision was and what I was going to tell him today. I then proceeded to say to him, "You need help. You can stay here for the time being." He cried. This man cried like a baby. I have never seen him in this state. Rob was a man who always played everything off; he was critical of others and often put people down. He was a hard-hearted man. To see him whimper as he did blew me away. I could not believe what was happening. With all this talk, and the shattered pieces of my heart, I had had enough discussion and confession. We ended the conversation; he went off to his fellowship, and I remained at home with the shattered pieces of my life.

So here I was, left with all this information of the secret life my husband had, with no one, except for God, to share it with. I journaled and reached out to God. For He, and He alone, could save me and comfort me at that time. I picked up that book Rob had given me earlier in the day. I opened it and started to read. I was taken back. *You mean to tell me my husband is not the only one with this problem? There are others? It's a sickness, an addiction?* Well, I felt like I was knocked over the head with a 2x4. I could not stop reading this book. It was giving me answers and knowledge that I was longing for; longing to understand. I read and read and read, and the best part about this book was that the morals and values it went by were coinciding with God. If this was what Rob was reading and starting to follow with the help of his new-found friends, well, to be honest, I was angry, resentful and so relieved at the same time. I spent the day reading that book, praying, crying and giving up my hold on this chaos. It was not mine to carry. For the first time in my life, I came to a place of, *What about me? Is there a place out there for me? A place where I can go to get help?* Funny that those questions arose in me. When Rob came home that night, he gave me a number. This number was for partners of people who are struggling with this issue. The following Monday, I called the number. I did not hear back. The following week I called again and again; no reply back. I did get discouraged, and I thought to myself, *Well, this must be God's way of saying to me that there's no need for me to call this number and speak to anyone.* Three weeks after my initial call, I received a telephone call back. The next day, I had a place to go. I was hesitant, but I was desperate. This was the end of June 2010.

As I think back to that day, I can only express gratitude for continuing to call and drag myself to where I needed to go. I experienced an overwhelming feeling of finding my way, finding a place; no, not just a place, but a family of people, with the same struggles that I was going through, welcome me with open arms and much love. God has provided a new family for me: a spiritual family. It's been a few years since God graciously led me to this family, and I have met the most fantastic people I will ever meet. I look forward to speaking with them each time I see them. And the most beautiful, humbling part is that I am learning and growing in Christ as I spend time with them. The amazing gifts I have received from these people, my new-found family, leave me in utter awe. How God's love has worked through them to chip away at my pride, ego, selfishness and "poor me" attitude has, in turn, brought me love for others in my heart. As I think about this, I'm stunned at the fact that, after all these years following Christ, I never had a heart for His people. I was full of hate and disgust towards human beings. I was unable to see them as hurting people who need God's mercy and love; and how could I give that if I never had it myself? God has been so gracious to me in extending His mercy and grace, and I just took, took and took with no regard of giving it away. I was selfish. I was unable to see this until God removed the "blinders" from my eyes and brought me to a place where His love was freely moving. For as long as I live, I will forever be grateful to my new family for showering me with these gifts.

So as I journeyed on in my life, for the first time in *my* life, I felt as though I was walking on thin ice ready to fall through the crack at any given moment. I took one day and one step at a time. As months went by, I slowly began to see myself for what I was. The mirror of myself was held up to my face. Oh boy, did God have a plan up His sleeve.

I'll be honest that, at first, I refused to see the truth about myself. I continued to think, *This is Rob's doing, not mine.* When I felt God afflicting me, I turned the focus on Rob, looked at and reminisced about all the "bad" things he had done and magnified his negative behavior to me and the family. I fought God on this for months until, one day, my oh my, I was knocked on my butt! Before this happened, I started to feel more and more empty inside. I became so much more critical, and felt like isolating more than I ever did in my life -- and I did. I did not sleep. I was getting to a point where I was seeing the "fruits" of my labour in our children. You see, over the years, I felt more competent and pulled together than Rob since *I* did the child rearing. God was graciously showing me what those efforts produced. What they produced in my children was hurt and pain; these "fruits" caused them to over-achieve in order to gain acceptance, look to drugs and boys to fulfill their emotional needs, self-harm, struggle with food, lose themselves in T.V. and isolate. It caused spiritual sickness in all three of them. I was not properly demonstrating the goodness of who God is. My words and actions did not match up. Why should they follow God if I continued to cling to old ways of behaving? I was not being a good representative of Christ; I was causing a mockery with my "I know all about God because I go to church and read the Bible" attitude. *Ha!* My children sought acceptance, and they tried to fulfil that longing -- a longing to be loved and cherished -- with worldly things. They were going down the same path Rob and I did at their age. As God afflicted me in this area, it was so powerful that it brought me to my knees. I brought this realization to my family who understood and, without judgement, loved on me and offered guidance.

With this loving guidance, I dove right in and started to take all my broken pieces -- that were "glued" together by *my* own ways -- apart. I let it all go, and *truly* offered and surrendered myself to God for the first time in my life. Now, let me be frank here: when I did this, I knew from previous experience in my life that this was not going to be an easy road. It was going to be a road mapped with hurts, sufferings and surrender of self. Was I ready for this? Heck no! But I buckled up and I pledged that I was going to enjoy the ride, for I knew that God had something remarkable waiting up the road for me if I stayed where He needed me to be. Remaining in this space of mind when things seemed to be getting on the right path was easier than when the waters got rough. This was a decision I needed to make on a daily basis; at times, it was one that needed to be made moment by moment. This took my walk with God to another level. I was letting go of *my* way of coping, which included anger, resentment and "putting up a wall" to keep others, especially Rob, out. I was unaware of how hurtful these behaviours were to my loved ones. I did not realize that giving someone the "silent treatment" or exploding at them in rage was harmful to our relationship, especially my marriage.

Keeping a distance from Rob was harmful to our marriage: it did not allow God's love to develop or grow. Instead, it did the complete opposite. With no room for God, our marriage was filled with pride, selfishness, ego, and someone, mostly me, in "power" of the other by picking out their faults and shortcomings. I was constantly nit-picking at Rob, comparing him to other men I knew, and hoping and wishing for him to have some of the character traits that these other men had. I prayed for Rob to change; I wished to be free from him, to find someone who would love me and respect me the way I deserved to be loved and respected. Well, what about the way *I* was treating Rob? Was this respectful? Was it honouring to him? Did I provide a place for him to feel safe to grow into the man God intended him to be? Or did I do the complete opposite? It took a lot of Christ in me to open my eyes to my part in the hell we were living. I was quick to blame Rob and his actions and behavior. To make matters worse, my part in his relationship with our children is devastating. My days of ranting and "bad mouthing" Rob in front of our children has made a very *big* impact on their relationships. Needless to say, there has been a rupture in the relationships Rob has with our children, and I have played a part in helping that along. Over the years, Rob's behavior would determine if I loved him, or if the kids should love and respect him (or even speak to him). The household ran on one condition: on the condition Rob was in when he arrived home from work. Once again, I set that tone in motion. Daily, when Rob came home from work, I immediately got my back up, became cold, quiet and refused to greet him at the door. The kids very soon picked up on their momma's treatment to dad. He became the "invisible" man in our home. It was me and the kids, and then there was Rob. The irony of all this is that I would fight with Rob about how he wouldn't be spending time with the kids and me, or have "family time" together with us. All the while, I was creating the division I did not want. I failed to see how my actions towards him affected our family, especially our marriage. I cannot begin to imagine how Rob must have felt coming home everyday. I cannot imagine how he felt with the rejection from his kids and his wife on a daily basis. I cannot imagine how it felt to feel like you were an outcast in your own home. Here I was just "fine": I had managed to create an alliance with my kids; I had "backup." I need to say how hard this was for me to admit to myself, to God and to my family. God worked with me through the years to open my eyes to see these hurtful behaviours, and He is still working with me today. These patterns of behaviours are embedded in me; through Christ, I am changing, and have changed, many of them.

I have also been made aware that these were ways of protecting myself from feeling hurt. These ways were *my* ways, not *God's* ways. I learned to treat others this way due to the hurt that I was caused in my life, and by my decision to not turn to God for Him to guide me through this hurt and heal my heart. This was all *moi*. Without God, I had no healthy way of dealing with heartache. It quickly turned into, "I will hurt you before you can dare hurt me." I lived a lifetime playing god. My efforts had produced more hurt and pain, and ruptured relationships. This was the "fruit" of my labor: pain and more pain. It wasn't until I became willing for God to work in my life and in this area of my marriage, and become more open and vulnerable, that I was able to step out in faith and trust God to do whatever He needed to do to change me from what I had created in myself. This did not happen over night, and I am still a work in progress, but great changes have taken place. When I am willing to let go of the wheel, God is able to move in my life. He brings me to such peace and serenity, and with that comes a time of emptying to grow. With all that I have been made aware of with Rob's past behaviours and choices, I always felt that I had a "right," a justification, to behave badly towards him. *After all, look at what he's done!* When I stay focused on that, I slip back to me. I don't like what *I* produce, I like what *God* produces in me. It wasn't until I accepted my behaviours as "not OK," and not "right" or Godly, that I was able to offer that to God and ask Him to help me become the woman He intended me to be. Not on condition of what others do to me, but on condition of who I want to be in Christ. For someone like -- me who's suffered at the hands of others and at my own doing -- continuing to change and do what is right for Christ (when I clearly see what's wrong), for me, takes much practice of facing the same obstacles and challenges in my life that arise. And truthfully, I manage to create my own obstacles when my focus comes off of God and myself, and is placed on others instead. This has been no easy task for me but I will share that, when I have victory, the incredible peace and growth and closeness I feel with my Saviour is unbelievable.

What I have learned to do is bite my tongue when I feel others are doing things "wrong." I've had to learn to mind my own business. I've had to learn to focus on what *I'm* doing and how *my* life is going; is it in accordance with God? What are the relationships in my life like? If they're not so great, what am I doing, or not doing, to help that? One important thing I've learned -- which is imperative with my changing and learning and walk with God -- is that, on a daily basis, I must make time for Him. I like doing this in the morning. I need to connect with my Maker, and seek Him early enough in the day to have Him set me on my feet. This takes discipline. As with anything else, I know that if I want a great relationship with my kids and husband, I need to put the time in, nurture that relationship, and get to know these people in my life. The same is true for my relationship with Jesus. There's no way I would know how to grow on my own, and I would not know His will for my life, if I failed to seek Him. This daily ritual started many years ago, and it has become the most important thing in my day. At first, I started with a half-hour of prayer and reading His word; and today, it goes from 1-3 hours. My strength through the hardships came from renewing myself with God everyday. There would have been no way I would be where I am today if God was not there. Over the years of journeying with God, He produced such strength in me and prepared me for what was to come in my life. He rid me of myself, and covered me from the inside out with Him. Only He could have known what was to come in my marriage and how we would get through it.

As Rob and I have worked out much differences, and have come to a place of forgiveness, of moving on and of re-commitment to each other, this has brought on a whole new set of challenges that were unexpected. To be honest, without realizing, I reverted back to a lot of old behaviour and ways of coping with what the Enemy has decided to throw on my plate. It's crazy: I've been faithful in spending time with God daily, and doing all the things I do to enhance my relationship with Him, all the while, quietly in the background, "I" was creeping out of the woodwork. I, not knowingly, started taking matters in my own hands.

I'll back up a bit. Rob and I have come a very long way

since his sex addiction has come to the light. We've been in "couple's therapy," and have started a get-together where couples who struggle with the same issue meet together twice a month. We've also taken some deep "couple's workshop courses" to get right to the "root cause" of a lot of issues we have. With all this, my perspective was, *Wonderful; we are really on the right track, and this time we are heading in the right direction. We are going to make it.* Sadly, there was too much of *us*, and not enough of God. That's the funny thing when you think you've reached a plateau: all is well, and the thinking comes to, *Yeah, I got this under control.* Then, *wham*, the carpet gets pulled out from under you. I have come to recognize these times as moments when God is continuing His work in my life. And in order for me to grow, it's going to be uncomfortable. At first, I resist and resist; I want my life to be just the way it was. I become angry and confused as to what has gone wrong and how I played a part in it all. I lash out and, with this latest incident, I reverted back to my old ways of behaving towards Rob. I'm talking the whole nine yards. Name-calling, shaming, getting the kids in on it. Boy oh boy, this behaviour was just itching to show itself again. It came out in full force.

This is what brought these old behaviours all about: after much therapy and "couple's work," we faced another obstacle very similar to what we had been dealing with (in regards to the sex addiction). This had been a devastation to me. Like

I said earlier, we were on the path of mending our broken hearts and getting help. We were praying together every morning, re-committing to each other and our marriage daily, and we had recently joined a weekly "couples' group." I truly felt that this was the last of our major issues. I was dead wrong. I cannot even begin to explain to you what happened here because, truthfully, I really don't know (which baffles me terribly). There was an incident one Sunday evening, and at first I felt that I could handle it calmly and lovingly (and it started off that way). That night, we slept in separate rooms. He provided very little, to no, explanation or remorse for what was done. I allowed how he was responding to the situation to affect me. I was getting very angry. I was confused and in a place of disbelief. *How could this be happening after the positive steps of action we were taking to prevent such a thing?* If there's one thing I have learned with my walk with God it's that, when temptation confronts you, you need to be truly armoured with God's "tools." This, I feel, needs to come from a place on the inside of you -- a place of wanting to truly be transformed through Christ. It's not easy, it takes time, and, from my experience, it needs to be done through God's Word and love. Only then will we be able to overcome what the Enemy places before us. Our flesh wants nothing more than to satisfy its own wants, regardless who it may hurt or destroy. That includes the destruction of ourselves as well. I had spent much time wishing and praying for everything to be OK. I knew that God was working behind the scenes on this one. He had it all covered; I just needed to be patient, quit asking, "why has this happened again," and stop trying to figure it all out. This is another prime example of *me* taking the wheel. Needing and wanting to know what is going to happen, and needing answers to questions I don't know. It had been hindering my connection with God; there was just way too much of *me* and not enough of *Him* in this picture. There comes a time when this way of carrying on comes to a halt for me. As I prayed and wrote in my journal, God was very gracious to lift the "blinders" off my eyes. My understanding of the emotional and spiritual sickness that haunts both Rob and myself was forgotten. My 1 Corinthians 13:1-8 love had became conditional again, and was replaced with hurt and anger. And with that hurt and anger came the ugly. The next few days, I shamed, ridiculed, yelled and, in my heart, was done with this person. By the end of the week, Rob left our home.

At first I had mixed emotions about this. I initially felt free, and felt like I could finally live my life in peace and without worrying about what Rob was doing, or who he was looking at, or whatever else he did. I felt free! Then, as a couple of weeks passed, I started to become very sad at what had happened to our family once again. Our kids had suffered and, this time, they were very angry. Their anger was completely justified; not only were we affecting our own lives, but we were also affecting the lives of our children. They will take this family experience, and it may damage them and their future relationships. This makes me feel angry and so disappointed in our efforts to get better. This pattern is a continuation in our marriage. I do suspect the breakdown comes from the lack of Godly wisdom and guidance in our marriage. When we fail to seek God first and foremost, when Rob and I tie ourselves together without God, and when we begin to lead the way by pushing God to the side and trying again (in our own efforts) to make things work, then our marriage experiences a breakdown.

I ask myself, *Why do I go back to that way?* The results that "my way" produces are damaging. It's not until I step back from myself -- from my emotions -- and look to what is really happening inside me, that I am able to come to a place of understanding what God needs me to see inside of myself and the nature behind behaviours (my own, as well as my husband's). Being willing to come to a place where I can evaluate the nature of my behaviour towards others, allows God to move in me. I am able to see, through the eyes of Jesus, the other person's hurt and deep-rooted pain. It is the pain and hurt that causes us to behave and look to things outside ourselves -- drugs, sex, alcohol, gambling, and conflict with others -- to fulfil that connection we are longing for. The very acts we commit to gain some acceptance, or love, do the complete opposite to our relationships. We unknowingly destroy the very thing we truly ache for. In my own experience, in order to protect my heart from hurt, I lash out and push the people I love away by putting myself above them, and by abandoning them; this way, I don't allow myself to become vulnerable. With this behaviour, I not only stop trusting God and miss a chance of growth with Him, but I also lose out on loving relationships with others. In short, I'm the one who sabotages my own life. I try to justify my behaviour by blaming and putting the focus and emphasis on, in my case, what Rob is doing or not doing. This kind of skewed thinking keeps the "road block" in our marriage.

And what's most important to me is where this leaves me with God. Does this behaviour line up with what God says? Does this behaviour serve me? Does it serve God? Does it serve the good of my marriage (which is a sacred vow to God)? How does this honour my spouse? This is what has become an important aspect to my life: honouring my spouse regardless if I feel he deserves it or not. And with that statement, I realize that it is nothing that we do, or don't do, that makes us deserving; we deserve because we belong to Almighty God. If my goal in this life is to love as Christ Jesus loves me, then my thinking on love needs to change. It needs to line up with God's thinking on love. Not this earthly love, but this Heavenly, Godly love that brings healing and restoration to the lives of others. When this becomes my main focus and goal in my day, I seek first my good Lord who guides me in the way to go. And I will say, the day does not come without its chance to exercise this love.

Since then, Rob has returned to our home, and, truthfully, the past year did not pass without much challenges. It seemed we were on this roller coaster that would not stop. Just when we thought we were on a smooth road, we lost sight of our Guide, and fell. The important thing here is that we get back up; we keep on getting back up and moving forward. Rob and I have come to understand that we both have issues -- past hurts and failures --- that we are working on, and that God is restoring in us; and through this restoration, He is bringing our marriage into unity with Him. We have together decided to surrender our marriage to Him, who is more powerful, to lead us and take care of us. God's plans, and His will for our lives, may not line-up with what we have planned, but we go along taking on what comes our way and accepting the path we are led down. There are times when we must get off a certain path to take care of ourselves, and, for me, this is another way how God works in me to help me grow. There is also an understanding that we are not here for the other to fix, mold or make new; instead, we have accepted that this is God's job. We have become willing to allow God to do His job. We need to listen and do His will for our life together.

One very important aspect to all of this is commitment. I

have lived my life with Rob with "one foot out the door." I would *say* that I was committed to our marriage; however, in my mind, there was always that thought of, *If he does this*, or, *If he does that*, and even thoughts of, *When I do this or that, I will be free*. With these thoughts, and that little "crack in the door," I was not fully able to be in this marriage and give of myself. It stopped God's plans, favour and blessings in our lives. If I was uncertain, how could God do His work? With this mind set, I was unable to move forward in my walk with God and my marriage. What needed to come to pass, what needed growing, was blocked due to my uncertainty. It was not until I was quiet enough to hear God speak to me, to feel His Holy Spirit move in me and bring this to the surface, that I have been able to fully enjoy the joy and peace He gives.

I can imagine some of you who are married may be experiencing the same kind of situations in your life. Growing a marriage in Christ requires *both* partners to be willing and fully committed to working on themselves -- their past hurts, abuse and trauma. Both partners need to have God as their first priority, and each other as second. Then come the kids. A family is only as strong as its weakest link. If the parents are not strong and fully committed to Christ and each other, this gives way to brokenness and instability in the family. When there is no stability in marriage and family, this does not create a safe place for anyone. There is also the concern of when a family is dealing with physical abuse. This requires some serious changes and help for those involved. Getting help for one's self is the start, and stops the cycle of continued hurt and abuse. Remember, change starts with us. In my experience, it has been a difficult journey to work on marriage with the effects of past abuse and trauma still lingering around. We all long for safety and fulfilling relationships.

The freedom and safety I longed for in relationship came from within me. It came from safety in God's arms. In God's mighty Hands. Trusting in Him, and placing my safety in Him, will be a journey that I will forever be on. This only comes from Him. God alone is the only One who can, and will, provide the love, safety and trust I crave in my life. To expect this from another human being leads me only to be frustrated and disappointed. The more secure I am in Christ, the more secure I am in myself. *I* is replaced with *Thee*. The more of me that gets cleaned out, the more room there is for Him who fills my life with such joy; a joy that is not easily shaken anymore. A joy that can only come from God. A joy that fills the depths of my being with peace and joy, despite external adversity and turmoil. This is a daily goal for me. Some days, I will be honest, I fail at tapping into the peace that is already in me. I get angry, I get frustrated; but I also recover from these feelings very quickly. At times, I act out on these feelings; and other times, I am able to accept life on life's terms and move on. None of this goes without a time of spiritual growing. This does not happen over night. Not even in a day, or a year or two. This happens with patience, and by going day-by-day, moment-by-moment, facing each challenge and hardship one at a time. It's in the "passing" of each hardship that we slowly begin to hold fast and change our behaviour to what aligns with God. *Our* ways and will start to move with *His*. It has taken me numerous times to "pass the test" on certain challenges in my life. I started to "catch on" to what was happening when I faced the same issues over and over again, and I reacted the same way over and over again. I was doing the same thing, reacting the same way and somehow expecting the situation to resolve in a more pleasant way. Finally, I "came to" and realized I needed to try something different. *My* way was causing the same insanity in my life, even to this day. God has called me to try things differently. He has even called me to change the ways that I often thought *were* His way, but really were not. God has shown me that, at times, standing up for myself and honouring myself is what He is asking me to do. He is also showing me to grow in ways of loving and respecting myself through continued hardships I come up against. Things are not perfect, nor will they ever be; but, I will tell you, there is more peaceful living. Yes, indeed. I have gained incredible courage and strength to move forward in my life. To go after what I want; and, if it is God's will, it will happen.

How do we know what God's will is? I can't tell you for sure. What I have come to know is that, when I feel alive and grateful, I know I'm in a place of goodness, and I know that I'm exactly where I need to be with God. What I have endured and experienced has opened new doors for me that I have never thought possible. The blessings I have received with writing and sharing are overwhelming. The trick to all of this has been sharing my experiences, and how those experiences have connected me with others. Some may have endured childhood sexual abuse; therefore, we can relate to each other. Some are teen moms; therefore, we can relate to one another. Heck, from one mom to another, we can relate. From a wife's perspective to another, we are able to relate. And, if we go deeper, from one human being to another, honestly sharing, we relate. I know what I have risen above was not for nothing. God had better plans for me. He knew one day I would be right here, right now, sharing with you that, no matter what, no matter what has ever happened to you, *you* will rise above it. *You* will come out on the other side better than you started. *You* will find others who can relate to your challenges; and by this, healing and restoration comes. You see, my friends, it is in giving away that we receive incredible gifts. I resolved long ago that, *I have a past, my past does not have me*! Friends, don't allow what happened, or what you may have done, hold you in bondage any longer. We, all of us together, make each other better. We offer a part of healing for one another by sharing our pain and knowing

115

we are not alone. Something miraculous starts to happen: we slowly move out of our isolation, and we start to fight against the chains that hold us. These chains of pain and our own imprisonment. We gain a new perspective on what we can do with ourselves, the dawn begins to break within ourselves, and we strive for a better life. We allow God to make our hardships our pathway to the peace only He can give. Our prayers begin to change, our focus begins to change and our thoughts begin to change.

I marvel at how the transformation happened. Bit by bit, day by day, discipline by discipline, behaviour change by behaviour change. Friends, this has not been easy. Me and discipline do not like each other. I use to be the type of person who did what they wanted regardless if it was right, wrong, or hurt anyone. I knew best. Especially with my history, I was not prepared to allow anyone, not even God, to tell me what to do. Anyway, as I became willing to give up *my* way and try *God's* way, a miracle happened. I call it a true miracle. With all the hurt and pain in my life, and how my prayers were so full of *me, me, me*, God healed my heart and soul. Through that, I am able to see the "silver lining" in *all* situations. And friends, let me share, this week has been like walking through fire for me. But guess what? I am coming out unharmed! And not to mention how the ability to tap into God's fruit of the spirit of self-control has saved me! Holy smokes! *Huge progress!* I'm thrilled at this one. It's been a tough one for me to break.

My prayers have changed: *Thank you, Lord, for this situation. I don't know why it's this way, but I trust You, and I know such goodness is going to come of it. I thank You for the work You are doing in me to draw me closer to You.* Yes, there were a few moments where I wanted to lose it, but guess what? I found healthier alternatives to release my rage: calling a few friends, praying, accepting my feelings and surrendering them to God by saying, *I'm powerless over my emotions. I know You can, and will, handle them for me.* Journaling is a big one for me. I also make sure to take time for myself -- I enjoy taking nice, hot baths, and taking time to just sit and listen to nature. I am able to enjoy the beauty right in front of me. I am able to take it in, breath deeply, and feel God's serenity come over me. When I get back to myself -- in the sense of being sure what I am doing, or not doing, "lines up" with God's word and what He asks of me -- then I know I will be OK. To do this, I need to be sure I am spending ample time with God; reading His word, and being quiet enough to listen for His voice. You see, I like to talk too much at times. I like to tell God all about what's happening in my life, how I don't understand things at certain times, and yadda, yadda, yadda. Then my prayer time and alone time with God becomes all about me. This breaks down the communication needed for me to hear what God needs to say.

We need to remember that it did not take us over night to acquire bad habits and faulty thinking about ourselves, and it certainly will not take a week or a month to change all of that. We do this one day at a time. We make small goals for ourselves, short term goals, and we reach them in our own time, in God's time. As we go along this path, it's important to keep the focus of where we want and need to go. Focus, focus, focus. Keep your focus on what matters, on what's good in your life. There will always be some instance or situation to ruffle your feathers, but, when we think about it honestly, will it matter tomorrow, next week, next year, or ten years from now? And if it takes us out of living in today, we are not truly living. And then who suffers? Our kids. Our families. *Ourselves*! Be free; focus on what's good. And if you are in a place of, "Nothing is good," well, friend, what *could* be good *right now*? When I feel "mushy," and I'm heading into self-pity, it's time for a "gratitude list" and a change in focus. There is so much good in life *right now*.

Life will never be what we expect it to be, and it will always have its challenges. That is life. Could you imagine if we all just went through life floating on a pink cloud? It would be nice for awhile, but how complacent would we get? We'd all be as if we were in "la la land," and our brains would certainly turn to mush! I could imagine it would get boring. And God did not design us this way. After the fall of man, God moved; He moved in a way we would never have been able to comprehend. He drew a plan. He walked with us. He made a way for us to survive and push forward. He offered us a gift. A gift we, at times, certainly don't deserve.

He has given us Grace through Jesus Christ. God's plan to save us from ourselves and the evils of this world was truly remarkable. To send His Son, Jesus, to save us from the evils of this world and ourselves. Grace is freely given to us no matter what we have done. God knows all about us. There is nothing we can hide from Him. He knows our sins, our failures, and He knows our heart. And you know what? He loves us anyway! He *loves* us anyway! He waits for us; He waits to hear from us to call out to Him. God loves us so much that He allows us to be free people; He allows us space to make our own choices and decisions. He knows we wrestle against the world and our flesh, and He knows what we are up against. And because of this, He never leaves our side. We may move away from Him when times get tough, but He is always there as soon as we call out His name. And when we do, He covers us with His love, mercy and grace -- free gifts, just because He loves us. We belong to Him. He restores what Satan takes from us. He moves in our lives when we least expect it.

Our job, my friends, is to break the chains of bondage. Whenever we feel defeated, that is our bondage; when we feel helpless, alone, unloved, and at our wit's end, these are our chains. When we feel self-loathing, self-hatred and low self-esteem, these thoughts and feelings are our bondage and chains within us. Our fear and distorted thinking of ourselves has come with years of wrong messages. It has come with emotional hurt, physical hurt and mental hurt. Sadly, other human beings in our lives suffer as we suffer. We must be able to look past that and know that these people in our lives have been hurt too. How we act towards others is a reflection of how we feel about ourselves. The driving force behind all of this is fear. Fear of rejection, fear of hurt, fear of being abandoned. God did not place this fear in us. This fear was cultivated and "grown" through bad experiences; through hurtful relationships and situations. It doesn't even stop there. Yes, we are aware of this fear and hurt, and, sadly, so many of us go through our life not knowing another truth. The truth is:

> *For God has not given us a spirit of fear, but of power and of love and of a sound mind* (2 Tim. 1:7).

Read that again. This time, replace the word "us" with *me*. For God has *not* given *me* a spirit of fear, but of *power* and *love* and a *sound mind*.

Believe it. These things are in *you*! Just because they feel trapped, doesn't mean they're not there. Make a choice to work this out in you. We *can* do it! I am living proof of it!

This has brought me to ask, What do you want? You want money? Start giving it away. Want extra time? Start giving your time. You want good kids? Be good parents. Stop criticizing your kids; accept them for who they are. You want good relationships? Be the good half of those relationships. Stop expecting your other half, or your friends, to do and be what you want them to be. Stop gossiping, stop judging, stop complaining. And, for crying out loud, stop being so hard on yourself! You want a fun life? Be fun yourself. Lighten up and stop taking yourself so seriously. Laugh, be silly, dance around, play with your kids, be a kid yourself. Want to hear from someone? Pick up the phone and make a call. Miss someone's company? Make arrangements to see them (if possible). Want a compliment? Give a compliment. Here's a good one: need a break or time for yourself? You have the power to give yourself that time. You want respect, forgiveness, love? Start giving it away. It will be uncomfortable, it will seem unfair. Please know, I do not suggest anything I have not done myself. Believe me when I say, Your life will change! It all starts right here, right now. It's all inside you. We have the power.

What does this do for us, and how can it help? As crazy as it seems, it helps by taking us out of ourselves -- out of our self-centeredness and out of our self-absorption. It amazes me how *everything* starts to fall into place when we take charge and make these bold moves. I will be very honest with you, I did not want to make changes like this. I felt that I had every right to be mean, complain, have this self-entitlement, and say, "What about me," "Why should I change," "I deserve better," "If they/he/she changes, I'll change," "Do you know what happened to me," etc., etc., etc., That, my friends, was driving me into a brick wall with all of my relationships, and I was constantly unhappy.

So how about, just for today, *we* make the change? Like Ghandi has said, "You be the change you want to see in the world." Start in your own little world at home. Choose one thing you can change today. You'll be pleasantly surprised at the response you get, and how you start to feel inside. That feeling is called joy. *Oh joy.* A bubbly, happy, loving feeling deep inside you. So, friends, let's try it today. Stop wasting any more time on what has happened to you, or what others are not doing for you. Get out there, break free and fill yourself with what God has given you: the potential to be the best you can be. He has empowered us with all that we need. Stop giving someone else your power. Give that power to God. Let's break free of the negative mind set that holds us captive. Let us walk forward in peace, choosing to forgive as He, Himself, has forgiven us.

You know, at the beginning of my journey walking with God, I never took into account that having an attitude of "poor me" was not pleasing to God. I did not consider the sinfulness of my bad attitude towards others and myself. I did not take into consideration when I said things like, "After all I've done for you," or "I can't believe you did that to me." These were selfish, self-centered and, I will add, quite self-righteous statements! When I think back to my old thinking and attitude like that, I chuckle at the sheer foolishness of it. I chuckle at how God must feel when I have done things that were not pleasing to Him. When I would continue on and on with the thoughts and actions of, *I'll take care of everything.* Giving Him the message that I knew better than Him. Yikes! It is easy to slip into this way of thinking, especially when things are not moving along the way we want. We "step in" to make things go our way, and try to get some results using our own efforts. What efforts do we use? Honestly ask yourself, What do I do to get things going my way? With others, do we use the "silent treatment" to let them know we are upset? Or how about "loving them to death" with "niceness" to hopefully produce some guilt in them so that they apologize or feel "bad" for mistreatment towards us? How about the "blame game"? Pleading our case for the other to see their wrongs? How about not truly living in your day? Our days are gifts to us. We have an opportunity, each new day, to live life to the fullest and make the most of it. In my previous years of "living life," I would say this with sarcasm. To truly live life, we need to take action in living. "Living life" are "action words" for me.

This is the day the Lord has made; we will rejoice and be glad in it (Ps. 118:24).

Had it not been for these "accidents" -- which, in my opinion, have been part of God's greater plan for my life -- I would not know how to "put the action" to the word, "living."

You see, I used to "live" life by merely existing in my day. Depending on what the days brought determined my moods, and how I behaved and lived. Me living my life rested in the "fate" and palms of others. Did others make me feel good? What could others do to make me happy and feel good? What were others doing in their lives that irked me, or made me feel right? Oh brother, this went on for quite a few years.

Today, thankfully, I know that living my life depends on me. Living right needs action from me. Changing my life for the better needs action from me. Growing in my life spiritually, mentally and emotionally needs action from me. I can sit around and wait 'til the "cows come home" for others to take action for my life and make it what I want, but that will never happen. This action, to live my life, is my responsibility. In order for me to have been able to take charge and take some serious action to start living my life, I first needed to depend on God. This amazing, gentle, compassionate, forgiving, loving God I have found, while going through hell, has been my source of strength. Without the relationship I have with Him, there would be *no way* that I would be where I am today. With His support, I have been able to truthfully acknowledge my shortcomings and behaviours towards myself, others and life. You see, if we don't know how we are operating in our lives, how we are treating others, and what we are thinking and saying to ourselves, we are unable to change the things that are holding us back from the goodness in life. Learning to love ourselves, and changing the hatred, anger, hostility, and resentment in our hearts, will open the doors to right living for us. I had no idea those were the very things stopping me from my best. After all, I had reason and justification for all those emotions, didn't I? Maybe so; however, it kept me down and very unhappy. Today, God continues to give me a transformed heart; and, let me tell you, He works on me daily to "take out" the ugly that still lurks inside.

I knew I could not have more of God inside me if I carried on with behaviours such as those. Through our journey growing in Christ, we will continuously encounter little "tid bits" of character flaws that need to be addressed. If our goal is to be more Christ-like daily, then we need change. We cannot continue unless we allow God to be the Lord of our lives. Growing spiritually requires the willingness to change and the learning to be faithful in the process. Mastering a new gift or talent requires patience and a consistency to practice. Behaviour change comes from within us. It first starts in our mind, and flows out into our actions and changed behaviour with each situation. Trust me, God will show you what needs changing, and He won't let you "off the hook" too easily. He loves us so much that He is willing to continue to mold us and fashion us into His beauty. To help me with this transformation and "clean up," I often go to a prayer,

God grant me the serenity to accept the things I cannot change; courage to change the things I can; and wisdom to know the difference. - Reinhold Niebuhr

How does this help me? Allow me to break it down.

God, grant me the serenity to accept the things I cannot change -- I realize I don't have the power in me, no matter what I say or try to do, to change people, places, things or my past. It took me many years to accept this fact. In the past, I believed that if I threatened, was aggressive, yelled, was louder than others, or had "things" my way, I was able to change outcomes and how others behaved. I bullied my husband and my kids into doing what I wanted them to do or behave how I wanted them to behave. This control over our kids, people, places, or things is an illusion. My eyes have been open to this false illusion. It's hurtful and damaging to relationships and to one's self.

Courage to change the things I can -- What can I change? Me, myself and I, and only that. For me, this courage to change needed much, much practice. So, how can we change the things we can? For one, we can try keeping defenses down. When we are in a discussion with someone, when there is conflict with someone or (good grief, here's a good one) when others are not doing things "our way," I have learned to accept their opinion and their thoughts. It doesn't mean I need to agree with them. It's a reminder that it is OK for others to live their life their way; it's OK for others to have their opinions. Second, I've learned to be a *responder*, rather than a *reactor*. We can only change ourselves; more specifically, our behaviour towards others and towards ourselves. We can change our attitudes towards people, places and things. We can change our thinking and, in return, change *our* life. And you know, it's funny because when I focus on myself and changing my life, regardless of what others are doing or not doing, everything in my life falls right into place.

Wisdom to know the difference -- This last part reminds me that everyone, every single person, has their own issues -- their own battles they fight within themselves. I have also come to know that, the more people lash out at me, or you, the more it is a sure sign that they are so unhappy with themselves. To understand and have compassion, instead of lashing back, has come with much transformation in myself. You can say I've had a heart transplant. With my own life's experiences and how I have harmed others with my behaviour, I am able, by God's Grace, to see the "why" behind the mistreatment people "dish out." I have to "step back and out" of my own emotions and not take it personal.

Sounds "hunky-dory" to be able to live this way, eh? I'll tell you, it has taken over fourteen years for this transformation to occur in me, and, to this day, I am still a work in progress.

For me, and maybe for you, it can start with one situation, one discussion, one day, one minute, one moment at a time to bring a different flavour to your relationships. Imagine if, when in conflict, we say, "Wow, sounds like you're in a tough place" (or something to that effect). Or how about just thinking about what kind of a life the person may have had. If I was given that consideration growing up, maybe, just maybe, I would have been… Nah, never mind, I wouldn't be where I am at this moment in my life had things gone differently for me.

Living this way has blessed me with an inner serenity. I still get "off track" from time to time, but the good news here is that this is a good indication and "barometer" of where I'm at with my spirituality, as well as with my mental and emotional health.

I have come to a great understanding and respect for my spiritual, mental, emotional, and even physical health. With God transforming my heart, a new-found love was created in me for myself. Staying connected to God daily, listening for His voice and reaching out and helping others maintains my spiritual health. Renewing my mind in His word creates in me a stable mentality which, in turn, gives my emotions balance.

> *And do not be conformed to this world, but be transformed by the renewing of your mind, that you may prove what is that good and acceptable and perfect will of God* (Rom. 12:2).

The incredible respect I have for my physical body today is truly remarkable. I know and understand that my body is the temple of God. He lives in me! God lives in me. And the more respect I have towards my Creator, the more respect I have for my own body -- I eat well, I exercise and I take time to rest.

Do you see what happens when we choose to want better for ourselves? All aspects of our lives change (like a domino effect). And where did this change first take place? In us. I read a saying once: *Change your thinking, change your life.* Those words couldn't be any truer for me. Friends, life doesn't magically become care-free or void of any obstacle or challenge, but it does become manageable, and our attitude towards each situation we face changes. We, in time and with devoted willingness, live happy lives.

Where has all of this left me with my children? These

relationships have grown so much, and I am still amazed at how I do not need to be the one to control the outcomes of their lives.

With God's transformation in me, I am a better parent. I love them better. I nurture them better. I am better to talk to. I am a better listener (OK, I struggle with this one at times). God has taught me to be a responder, instead of a reactor, when interacting with my children. He has graced me with the ability to accept them as individual people -- His people, His children. He has taught me to put myself in their shoes and use my ears for listening to them (instead of simply hearing when they speak). He has led me to be curious about what's going on in their lives. How has this happened? I have accepted that God is their Father -- He has a Hand in their lives. He loves them and will never forsake them, just as He has never left or forsaken me. These children were given to me "on loan" from God. He has entrusted me to be a godly mother to them. I now know what my goal is regarding being a parent: for me, it is to live a godly life honourable to God. It is to bring my children up in the Lord, and guide them with godly principles to go along their life.

Some may ask, How do you expect teenagers to listen to you and that "stuff"? In my experience, in order for teens to listen, a foundation and a relationship needs to be set when they are younger. It needs to be a foundation that offers respect and unconditional love. I also believe that it is important for a parent to show respect for themselves as well. How a parent nurtures and respects themselves shows their children that they are of value. It's never too late, or early, to instill these behaviours in yourself or your children. I recall a bedtime routine I started when my kids were very young. This routine consisted of reading a book, chatting about the day, and something that I believe has helped them accept and find love inside themselves: the kids needed to tell me something special about themselves. Something they liked about themselves, something they accomplished. This "something special" needed to be new every night. It was a routine that lasted many years. To this day, when we have family nights, we sometimes incorporate this routine again and add into it something special about each family member. My favourite "special thing" they would often share was, "God loves me." When I heard those words come from my children, my heart was full of delight.

My kids and I share in a very good relationship today. I am often amazed at how blessed I am with the relationships I have with each of them. They are all different, yet the same in many ways. We still have our times of trouble, but the fact always remains the same: you are loved no matter what. It is possible to share in wonderful relationships with your kids, even after feeling as if you've done so much damage to the relationship. I am living proof of that. I have had to be consistent and know that these relationships are important, and as I have learned to make amends to them, I must carry out my living amends with how I behave and speak towards them. It does not matter what the situation is, for God has His Hand in it. Our part is allowing Him to move in our children's lives and trusting that He will make everything work out for our benefit. I do this on a daily basis. Just for the day I am in, I am going to trust and believe that God is working in my favour. And guess what? He is! And all the while He has been teaching me patience, and guiding me to grow in my faith and trust for Him.

One thing is for certain: God's love never fails. It is truer as the day He created us. He will never run out on you. He will be faithful to you in all you do. What we ask and plead God for in times of heartache and trouble may not always seem to be answered. But God knows best. He knows what is good for us; just as those of you with children know what is best for your child, so, too, does God know what is best for His children. He may not give us what we ask, but He will never leave you with what you don't need. Allow Him to take charge, to guide you. God will never allow you to go where He cannot protect you. All things will work out for your good. I say this with the utmost confidence because I have seen the goodness, I have felt the love and I have tasted the goodness of The Lord. Break every chain that holds you;

Jesus has the power. He has the ability to make all things new and restore in us what the Enemy has taken from us.

So I will restore to you the years that the swarming locust has eaten... (Joel 2:25).

So, as I come to the end of sharing my journey with you, I am reflecting on where my life is today. I believe I am entering a new season of my life. There are many things that are still very familiar, and I continue to struggle through some of the same issues. Rob and I? Well, this marriage -- this relationship with ourselves and God and each other -- will be a continuous endeavour. Just this past weekend we got into a situation, and now, a few days later, we are back at it, picking up the pieces. I accept the fact that challenging times are an opportunity for me to grow, for our marriage to grow. We must face some obstacles; if not, we stay complacent.

Living and being together requires us to love one another and help each other recover from past abuse and unfinished business. This needs to be a goal for *both* partners to ensure the success of the marriage. Effort from both sides needs to be a priority in order for the marriage to work. I can not stress this enough. Friends, it also means that, if you're partner is not putting in the effort, *you still can!* You can still work on yourself to be who God intended you to be. We don't place the fate of our lives in another human being's hands; no, we place that fate in the Mighty Hands of God. I can relate to how heart breaking it feels when your marriage is not at its fullest potential. I can relate to how difficult it is to push forward when you feel as if you're leaving something, or someone, behind. The fact and question remains: what do you want for your life? Are you getting it? Are you doing all you can in your relationship to make things work? And here's a good question that I've asked (and have had to answer honestly): are you doing too much in your relationship to make it work? Any relationship takes more than one person to nurture it, and this is very true for marriage. I held myself so accountable over the years for not being or doing enough, and the truth was that *I* was "in the way." When we are constantly trying to make things work, we block out God's plan and will for us and the other person involved. There comes a time when we need to learn healthy boundaries and allow God to do His work. I have found this exceptionally difficult in my marriage. I am walking through this process these days, and it feels strange and empowering at the same time. Relationships will always be a work in progress, just as we are ourselves. I love to say, "Marriage works if you work it." And that's just it: we can't just sit around and wait for our partners to get moving; no matter what has happened in our marriages or relationships, we have a part. If we are willing to put our pride aside, we can enjoy the best life our Creator has intended us to live. We gotta do our part so that He can do the rest and meet us half way.

Thinking back to my earlier years, if anyone had said these words to me or suggested I try "this" or "that," I could honestly share, there would have been no way I would dare be the first one to make the move. And I also know that I placed a lot of blame on my partner. It was easier to do that instead of taking responsibility for my part and behavior in my life. It was very easy for me to magnify Rob's behaviour instead of my own. And as long as I focused on that, we lived an awful life together. What harm has it caused for me to take the initiative for a better life? None. In fact, it has freed me to become a better person and stop using my past abuse as an excuse -- a crutch -- to stay miserable or "stuck." There is no doubt that my past abuse reeked havoc (and still continues to try to) in my life, but there came a time for me when, by the Grace of God, I was able to face that demon and move forward. The effects of the sexual abuse will try to creep up when I encounter trials and situations, but, being aware of what they are, I am better able to change my behaviour and ways of dealing with others and myself.

Yes, trials and challenges will always be -- that is a part of life. But they are of no comparison to the love I feel from God, and the incredible joy and peace I am able to maintain and live with today. I have seen many glimpses, and felt many moments, of true unity with my husband. I truly believe what we have endured together, as a couple, has made us better friends, lovers, and husband and wife. It took the real nasty to get us to return to one another and find out what true love is: God's love. This kind of love is cultivated, grown and practiced until it becomes part of your transformed heart and life. It took some time for us, and I believe it will take more time. And I'm sure we are not free from future challenges and situations, but what I do know is that we can overcome them. For Christ said, "...with God all things are possible" (Matt. 19:26). And that is the truth for me. There is no way that I could have gotten through what I went through, and be where I am today, had it not been for my God. I know that Rob and I could not have overcome what we have faced in our marriage had it not been for the grace and mercy of our Lord, Jesus Christ. Our family would not still be together had it not been for the Mighty Hand of God holding us together. And for this, I am eternally grateful and forever humbled.

The love and attention I had so desperately craved in my earlier years has been so filled with the love of God. I no longer need another human being to fulfill my needs of attention or love. The incredible overwhelming power of love that comes only from God has sustained me and given me such a peace that I have never known. If I had the chance to change anything about my past, would I? No. No, I wouldn't, because the gift I have found through this life has been far greater than I could ever comprehend! And if this is what needed to happen for me to be where I am today, so be it. God's will is God's will. And I know, in my heart, His plans are never to hurt or harm me. They are to always give me a hope and a future. The trick here has always been my surrendering to Him, my willingness to want to get well and the questioning of my willingness to want to get well. I will go through my days knowing that God's work in me is not done. And I will keep the attitude of faith, and hold myself steadfast to take on challenges with Him by my side. For with Him, I can, and do, get through it all.

My prayer for you is this,

I pray that your heart is opened no matter what you face, be it with your partner, your children or yourself. I pray that you know that God has never left you or abandoned you, and that He never will. I pray that you call out to Him. I pray that you begin, in this very moment, to see yourself and your life in a new light; a light that reveals how God is working things out for you. I pray that you ask Him what it is that *you* can do to be the change. I pray that you ask Him to heal your heart; that you ask Him to come into your heart and heal you from the inside out. I pray and ask this in Jesus' Powerful, Mighty Name. Amen.

I know this is not the end; this is just another beginning to another chapter of my life. You see, my kids are heading into their adulthood. One of them is already there. I suspect that this journey for them has taught them and opened their eyes to the undeniable power of God. I also imagine that it has given them insight into what to be aware of with their relationships, and how important it is to have a spiritual foundation to fall back on. I look forward to seeing God's plans unfold in their lives.

Hug your children and hug yourself today. Enjoy the day, the minute, you are in. You are here! You are in this moment. You're awesome, beautiful, amazing self is in this moment!

Bloom where you are planted today, and know that you are exactly where God needs you to be at this very moment. Nothing, absolutely nothing in God's world, happens by mistake.

I feel overwhelmed as I come to the end of this book. I started it over three years ago, and here I am with the last finishing touches. I thank all of you for journeying along with me. May God bless you and keep you. May His face shine upon you always. Remember that, no matter what comes of each day, you can get through it. There is not obstacle too big for God, and if it is God that goes before you, who dare be against you (Romans 8:31).

I urge you, get yourself a great version of the Good Book if you haven't gotten one yet. Start reading -- even start with just five minutes a day -- and I guarantee, the changes will come. Changes for the better. You will feel a peace like no other peace. And let me tell you, whatever you may have done in your life, or whatever may have happened to you, God loves you today more than ever. There is nothing we can do, or not do, to make Him love us any less. God never leaves our side. We may, over time, move away from Him and wonder why He left us; but, truth be told, we left Him. There is no better time than now to return back to Him. Get to know God for who He really is; not who religion says He is, but who His Word says He is. Find out for yourself, just as I did.

As you continue on your own journey of life, know that you can make it. Be true to yourself and love yourself. The more we learn to love ourselves, the more love we give to others, and we become all that we are meant to be. Make today, whatever day it is, be the start of a new way of living, a new way of thinking, and a new way of treating yourself. Today is a great day. Count your blessings as you come to the end of reading this book. Heck, even that could be an accomplishment! There is beauty and blessings and gifts all around -- take them in. Vow to start each day with gratitude. For today is a new day, a new start to the rest of your life. Break the chains that hold you. Get out there; what you have will benefit others. Get out there and live with purpose and passion. God has great plans for you -- go and take His promises for your life! They are yours!

Epilogue

It is May 2013. It's been another challenging year. My husband and I have met, yet again, more challenges. Our relationship has hit a block that cannot be moved at this time. I'm feeling quite numb today. For weeks I've been praying and asking God, *Lord, what is it that you need me to know with this situation?* Today, I believe I heard Him. Addiction is a very cunning and baffling disease. When one suffers with addiction, there is already a set of challenges; throw mental health issues in the mix, and we've got an ugly mess on our hands. For myself, I have sadness; and, at the same time, I have come to accept that what we are dealing with goes far beyond addiction and with that, we do the best we can to go through each day together. I have finally been able to accept this reality, and focus on myself and what is right and just for me. I know in my heart that there is nothing I can do, or not do, to change anyone else except me.

I love my husband. I love him very much. I have seen such

goodness in him; a goodness that reminds me of when I first met him and believed he was my knight in shining armour. He has always provided for us. He has given me the space for me to work on this project regardless of what was happening between us. I will forever be grateful for this. I will forever be grateful for the lessons I have learned through the journey I have been on with him and the future lessons we will learn from one another.

What can I say about living with addiction? It's sad. It's hurtful. It's damaging. Not only to the people who love the one who suffers, but it's even more sad to watch the one who suffers from it. There's a feeling of helplessness and loss of control. There's also those feelings of feeling crazy yourself! It is a feeling of being pulled under water while fighting to stay afloat. It's frustrating trying to explain to others, and even to yourself, what you're living with when no one believes the insanity and that we too are part of the insanity that goes on. I have grieved that my kids have suffered the effects of addiction. I can only imagine what they must feel and what goes through their minds. I can only imagine the pain they feel. The abandonment they feel. The loss they feel. And as a family, we grieve the loss of unity and fellowship together.

This is a new venture for me, and I know Who goes before me as I step out. There came the feelings of "going backwards in my life," but I was gently reminded that I could, instead, see this as a new beginning. A beginning that God is writing for me. A new life, rising above the pain, heartache and abuse that the effects of addiction and mental health have left in their wake.

I am excited to see what God has prepared for me. I know that He would not take me this far just to leave me. He has never failed me before, and I don't believe He would start now. I do have faith all things will work themselves out.

As for my relationships with my parents and siblings? I am very pleased to note how much understanding and compassion I have gained towards them and myself. There was a time when I stayed completely away from my family of origin. I did not visit, call or keep in touch with any of them. I now know that this was a time that was needed for me to be in a safe place to work on my abuse and the effects it had taken on my life. It was a very lonely time, but it was much needed. And it was OK to take this time. I see the benefits of letting things begin with me. I held onto a lot of resentment and hurt growing up with my family of origin. Letting go of those feelings enabled space for new, healthier relationships to grow. Offering forgiveness where it was needed and allowing God to fill that hole of hurt and loss has helped me become a better person. I am more comfortable visiting my parents and sharing openly with them. I am more free to visit my siblings with understanding of myself and them. I understand that we all have suffered the effects of addiction and dysfunction, and I remember that we are all doing the best we can. What's important for me is to always focus on what *I* am doing and not doing. This includes minding my own business, as well as not discussing personal affairs of family members when they are not present. It also includes taking time to pick up the phone to call my family and "stay in touch" (this is an area I continue to work on as isolation is my "favorite" thing to do). I will gladly share that I recently took a bus trip, with my kids, to my sister's place (which is an hour away). Yes, there was a brief moment of "disturbance," but I walked through it and had a great time. I also answer the phone when someone calls me, whereas before I would have avoided talking on the phone as if it was the plague! My brother and I were visiting one day, and he was upset about something. He asked me about the situation, and I merely shrugged my shoulders and had no opinion on the matter. He replied to me, "Chris, can't you be like you were a few years ago and freak out about this?" I said, "Nah, I'd never go back there." I was pleased with my change of response and feelings towards a situation that had nothing to do with me, and I was pleased that my brother saw a comparison in my response. It made me feel that I have changed. Changed for the better. I am nowhere near perfect, and I wish to not ever reach perfection until the day I meet my Maker.

I will share with all of you that I have decided to make

contact with my abusers; I have decided to go forth and confront them. At first I contemplated sending a letter, but I decided that I now possess the courage to call them on the phone. I had called a few times and left messages, but, to no surprise, there has been no reply. Could they possibly know why I am calling them after all these years? With no response from either of them, I was led to mail them a letter the good ol' fashioned way. Hand-written, stamped and put in the mail box. It took about a week before I heard anything back. Sadly, those letters got into the wrong people's hands. Other family members opened my abusers letters and read them. When I did hear back, it was not from my abusers, but from their mothers. In fact, it was not even me who heard from them, but my poor parents who had no clue of what was coming their way. From what I heard, there was some heavy reactions and denial. To be expected, yes. I believe this is the beginning to an end of the horror this abuse has caused in my life. I feel confident and pleased with myself for confronting them. In my opinion, it turned out rather unfortunate for my abusers, because their families exposed them openly. They shared who they are and what happened. Those letters were supposed to be between me and my two abusers, not their families. I am reminded, through this ordeal, that nothing happens in God's world by mistake. If having my abusers exposed is God's way of saving others, or even these men, then so be it. God's will is never wrong. Ever.

145

So, as it stands today, the "secret" is all out in the open. I no longer carry the shame or pain of what happened. I am in total awe at the God-given confidence and strength that has been activated in me. The incredible healing of heart, mind, body and soul is so freeing. Where this situation will lead, I do not know; but, I do know that what I did was right and just for me, as well as for anyone else who may have been hurt. I have Almighty God to thank for this.

Confronting them has brought up some unsettling feelings for me. I seem to be reflecting on the effects of what I have been left with all my life after what their actions have done to me. Maybe they, too, have both suffered as I have over the years. I imagine that they have suffered with guilt, shame or maybe even the effects of this abuse on their own lives. Maybe their lives keep hitting brick walls and road blocks? Maybe their relationships with their significant others reek havoc and continue in sheer dysfunction? Yes, I want to rant. I want to say to their faces, "How *dare* you? I want to show you what your actions have done! I want to yell and scream at you! I want you to *know* that this was not OK. Not *ever*! And don't you dare greet me with a hug or with an attitude like nothing happened!" How awful I lived my life not knowing what kind of a person I was. To allow abuse and mistreatment *all* my life because of someone else's bad choices and actions towards me. *Never again*! Today, I say, *Never again*. Not from anyone. I have choices now. God has restored in me what was taken, and He continues to restore in me what He has planned for my life.

We are all precious. We all start off as children and become adults. Some of us, who have been abused, end up staying little children inside adult bodies until we face our demons and work through trauma. Stuffing, suppressing, repressing and minimizing past abuse does not make any of the effects go away. In fact, as I said before, the effects come "sneaking out" into our relationships, damaging and reeking havoc in their path. It is truly a sad thing. I know there are so many survivors out there who are so scared to even "come out" and share their abuse, or even admit to themselves that they encountered such abuse at the hands of another. I was one of them. To face the effects of the sexual abuse I endured as a young child was heart wrenching. But friends, I cannot tell you enough how free and how much self-love and *respect* I have gained for myself through God's love and healing in my life. I can also tell you that it has been the best therapeutic healing I have ever received. The bondage that the abuse puts on our souls begins to loosen, and our souls begin to feel freedom; we eventually learn to forgive ourselves, accept what happened, and gain so much understanding as to why our lives took the turns it did, and even why we have chosen partners in our lives who could not love us the way we needed in order to heal. I urge you, my fellow survivors, to share your story -- you were made for great things. Don't allow the Enemy, who belongs of this world, to hold you down any longer. Do not give your abusers your power. Own it, and live your life. Stop cowering down, and face yourself and your life. Do not come to the end of your life with a "wish list" and "if only's." You owe this to yourself. Break free! You can do it!

When I was a young girl, my mom gave me a book of *Psalms*. I used to sleep with that book under my pillow. Over time, I had memorized "Psalm 23." I would repeat this psalm over and over in my head as I went to sleep. During the wee hours of night, when I would awake in fear, I would call out to God and recite this psalm.

Throughout this journey, I was reminded of this psalm. I re-read it, took the words of the psalmist David to my heart, and understood it in a different meaning this time. Being so young, I could not comprehend the words of this psalm fully. Today, I can see through these words, take them into my heart, and fully understand them. I'd like to share this psalm with you.

"The Lord is My Shepard"

The Lord is my shepherd; I have everything I need. He lets me rest in green pastures. He leads me to calm water. He gives me new strength. He leads me on paths that are right for the good of his name. Even if I walk through a very dark valley, I will not be afraid, because you are with me. Your rod and your walking stick comfort me. You prepare a meal for me in front of my enemies. You pour oil on my head; you fill my cup to overflowing. Surely your goodness and love will be with me all my life, and I will dwell in the house of the Lord forever (Ps. 23 New Century Version).

To explain how this psalm resonates with me is as so,

The Lord is my shepherd; I have everything I need -- The Lord is my guide, my protector. He ensures my *needs* are met, not my wants (though He gives me those too, at times). I will not go without. Just as a sheep is taken care of by the shepherd, so am I taken care of by my Lord.

He lets me rest in green pastures. He leads me to calm water -- Whatever trials I go through, He is leading me to a restful place. He guides me to where the calmness of life is, and, for me, that is in Him.

He gives me new strength. He leads me on paths that are right for the good of his name -- Through the trials and challenges of life, He renews in me new strength, new courage and new

149

resiliency to keep moving forward. To keep pushing forward towards His glory. He turns me towards His goodness, and reveals in me what is right and just for Him.

Even if I walk through a very dark valley, I will not be afraid, because you are with me. Your rod and your walking stick comfort me -- I cannot begin to fathom how I made it through some years of my life. Reading this line in the psalm reminds me that it was God who was right there beside me. Just as I have come to the challenge of confronting my abusers, I was not afraid. Why? Because He has been right alongside me, guiding my steps as I have gone along. It does not mean that I don't ever get afraid; those feelings creep up, but I am reminded, and I now know, to call on Jesus and remember that He goes before me.

You prepare a meal for me in front of my enemies -- This makes me feel like our Lord has made a way for me. He shows the goodness that comes out of harm done to me (by others or myself). Although negativity or harm may come my way, God will provide for me, in the light of my "foes," His mercy and goodness.

You pour oil on my head; you fill my cup to overflowing -- He pours oil on my head. This is significant to me because it symbolises, for me, that God has anointed me: He calls me His own. He fills my cup. When I am empty inside, when I feel vacant, He fills my soul. He fills my heart with love, and renews in me a new strength.

Surely your goodness and love will be with me all my life, and I will dwell in the house of the Lord forever -- As I dwell with God, live my life towards Him, and come to know Him more, His goodness and His love will chase me down. It does not exempt me from trials, but it reassures me that His goodness and love will always, and forever, be with me for the rest of my days.

This will not be the last of me. No, no, no. I plan on doing great works for The Lord. I look forward to the rest of my days serving and growing in Him. I look forward to, as crazy as this sounds, the next set of challenges that may arise, for I know the gifts and spiritual growth that comes from them. I look forward to what this book has prompted in your lives. I look forward to each new day as an opportunity to live with God's passion for life and serve.

As I have said before, sharing my experiences, and how those experiences have connected me with others, is miraculous and joyous. By all of us working together, we have created healing, relationship, and connection. And friends, this connection is all over the world!

I know what I have risen above was not for nothing. God had better plans for me. He knew that one day I would be right here, right now, sharing with you that, no matter what, no matter what has ever happened to you, *you* will rise above it. *We*, all of us together, with God, make each other better.

Be bold, get out there, and let's show others that God can do anything!

God bless.

CPSIA information can be obtained at www.ICGtesting.com
Printed in the USA
LVOW11s2309230215

428028LV00005B/43/P